Mimi Wellisch was born in Hungary a few years after World War II. Her mother was a survivor of Auschwitz and Buchenwald concentration camps. As a 7-year old Mimi fled to Denmark with her parents during the Hungarian Revolution. There, she attended school and met the love of her life at the age of 15. The relationship was interrupted when her parents decided to migrate to Australia where she met her first husband. Years later, on a trip back to Denmark, Mimi met up with her childhood sweetheart again. Her memoir is about their passionate, tempestuous and enduring love.

Once Upon a Love

Mimi Wellisch

First published by CKC Sydney in 2021
This edition published in 2021 by CKC Sydney

Copyright © Dr Mimi Wellisch 2021
Edited by Gail Tagarro
http://cleverkidsconsultancy.com
The moral right of the author has been asserted.

All rights reserved. This publication (or any part of it) may not be reproduced or transmitted, copied, stored, distributed or otherwise made available by any person or entity (including Google, Amazon or similar organisations), in any form (electronic, digital, optical, mechanical) or by any means (photocopying, recording, scanning or otherwise) without prior written permission from the publisher.

Once Upon a Love: A Chance Encounter in Copenhagen

EPUB: 9781922389718
POD: 9781922389725

Cover design by Red Tally Studios
Note: Some names have been changed to protect privacy

Publishing services provided by Critical Mass
www.critmassconsulting.com

Front Cover Photo: Viggo, 16, in Mimi's room, drying his wet clothes in front of the radiator, November 1964.

Back Cover Photo: Mimi, 15, with her guitar in her room, 1964.

My relationship with Mimi has been like a spiritual journey, because that's what it's like when you really love someone

—Viggo Knackstredt, 20/12/2017

DEDICATION

To my grandchildren Veronika and Hannah who always said: 'Tell us the story again about how you met'; and to the other grandchildren, Annika and Emilia, who were too young to ask.

CHAPTER 1

Doctor Death is knocking on the open door to Viggo's room, his raised arm revealing a dark blue semicircle of sweat. I don't remember his real name. It's the nickname the family gave him the moment we first saw him. I know it sounds unkind, but with his overly polite manner and condescending smirk he seems untrustworthy. His dark hair is always slightly greasy and although he is neatly dressed, he gives the impression of being slovenly. There is even something creepy about him.

It is an apt nickname, as he is the resident doctor at the palliative care unit.

Without waiting for permission to enter, he oils his way into the room. His offsider soon joins him on their daily rounds. A nurse follows with a rattling computer trolley, barring the doorway.

We both look up at Doctor Death expectantly, Viggo in bed, leaning back against the pillows, and I from a standard issue tan vinyl armchair beside him. Neither of us ever dreamt that our first electric meeting and much later passionate affair would eventually lead us here.

After a few polite enquiries, the doctor launches into a quiet, droning, heavily accented monologue about how palliative care units are meant for short-term stays, and that patients rarely remain much longer than four weeks. Then they thank Viggo for his time, turn, and head out to see the next patient. They leave behind a feeling of dread and a sense of reproach that Viggo isn't doing a good job of dying within the allotted time of their policy.

Despite this, the doctors have themselves been complicit in this outcome. I have been watching them for several weeks now patronisingly humour Viggo's own belief in his recovery by agreeing to treat him with medication, blood transfusions, and intravenous fluids—although they never fail to remind him that he can stop the treatments at any time. We all have a role to play in this bizarre pantomime. The doctors oblige with treatments while at the same time, they are waiting for Viggo to be ready to die. Viggo plays the invincible hero, denying the inevitable. And I am the long-suffering, grieving wife. We all know there is only one possible outcome, despite the treatments that are slowing down the process, so now I may have to look for alternative care for him. A nurse has mentioned a nursing home, but I can't do that to him.

My mind feverishly searches for a solution. Perhaps, somehow, I will be able to nurse him at home. Nicola, our daughter, desperately wants him to have the very best death possible. But she is working and he is so frail now that it requires two adults to turn him every few hours to prevent bed sores. Besides, making changes to his situation at this time requires energy, and I am depleted. I wonder how much a private nurse would cost around the clock, and even how to find one. Perhaps there is an agency somewhere. We can probably afford it, depending on how long …

A similar scene played out a few weeks ago, before Viggo was transferred here from the main hospital. There, too, doctors had held out hope for him, prescribing a trial medication and other treatments—while slowly introducing the frightening idea of palliative care. They said it was up to Viggo how long he wanted to fight on. However, it eventually came to a head and by the time his specialist filed into Viggo's room with his entourage for the last time, my darling husband had fallen out of bed several times, been revived by a huge response team, and had at least 50 accidents in bed. His specialist looked at him gently and then, in what seemed like a rehearsed speech, told Viggo that unfortunately they were unable to do any more for him. They had run out of treatment options, but it had been a privilege to be his physician and he wished him well.

Viggo looked up from his bed with pleading eyes and asked, 'Does this mean that I am dying?'

There was an almost audible communal intake of breath in the room, and then the doctor said, 'Yes, I'm afraid so.'

The words hung in the air amongst us all—my brother John who had come to visit, my daughter Rebecca, our children, Joshua and Nicola, and me. An almost surreal timelessness ensued in the wake of the words we had all expected and feared. Our eyes were fixed on Viggo's face for his reaction, yet it felt so voyeur-like, as if we had somehow intruded unintentionally and overheard a very private conversation.

After that, things moved quickly and within days, Viggo and I were in a patient transport vehicle on our way here. I held his hand all the way, squeezing it gently in the hope I could reassure him, aware that this would be his last ride, at least while he was alive. That night I slept on a low camp bed next to his high metal one so he wouldn't be frightened. As I fell asleep, I wondered how many people had previously died in that room and awoke several times from nightmares filled with horrifying images. After a few days, when the doctors had spoken of possible improvements and even told us about people who had returned home from palliative care, I decided to go home to sleep. It was a lot more comfortable, although I kept worrying that maybe he couldn't reach the buzzer, or maybe he felt abandoned, and the first thing I did each morning before returning to see him was to call the nurses and find out whether he had had a good night.

However, one day after leaving his bedside briefly to get some lunch when he was napping, he became distraught upon waking to find that I had gone, and I realised that it was time for me to stay and sleep on the camp bed again.

So, this private room with the number 16 on the door and the ensuite bathroom is our last shared home, albeit a temporary one.

There is a rhythm to the days. I wash and hang to dry my spare T-shirt and undies while the nurses wash him. The remaining time is one long continuum, punctuated by doctors' visits, frequent requests for bed pans, medication, long periods waiting outside his room until the nurses have dealt with his toileting yet again and cleaned him up, mealtimes, and phone calls and visits from friends and family. In between, when we are alone, there descends a silent tenderness between us. Our eyes lock in loving exchanges. Our fingers gently stroke and smooth out each wrinkled line on our hands. There is plenty of time to revisit the past, although Viggo no longer feels the need to confess events that have caused him pain or that he feels guilty about. That happened four years earlier when he had his transplant.

He was very sad at the time, had many regrets and tears. I had read that happens when someone is about to face death. But he survived that episode. This time it is more about *us* making peace with the past, something we must come to terms with together. Each of us has a stake in examining, weeding out, and bundling up the past that we co-created. So we discuss our tempestuous relationship; we are awed yet again as we dissect our courageous and repeated choices to be together despite insurmountable barriers; we tell each other how proud we are of our children, how proud we are of all we have achieved; and we talk about our regrets, the people our relationship hurt along the way. Viggo is especially sad about the pain he caused his first wife, Gilla. I see it more as destiny, and offer him the solace that it was 'meant to be'.

I have been grieving since Viggo was diagnosed almost 14 years ago. So now that he is finally dying, I'm beyond tears, numb, doing whatever is necessary in a semi-automatic state. He and his needs are currently the content of my life. My sole purpose is to wait with him, patiently be there for him. It is so unlike the old me. Mastering patience has been a long, steep, learning curve, enabled by a million disappointments, endless hours waiting for doctors' appointments, and a final surrender to the infamous 'hospital time'—all these ransoms, in exchange for more time with the love of my life.

There is no future now. We look forward only to the emergence of each new, precious moment. I am ready for him to die, having lived for years on high alert, through one health emergency after another, each different and even more shocking than the last, yet somehow always unexpected. During this time, I have become an expert in his rare blood disorder, and an unwilling witness to how it has ravaged his body ... his beautiful olive-skinned body, so innocent, so delicious, before the onset of the angry rashes, the welts and lumpy scars from procedures and operations. So perfect before the bruises from a million blood tests, cannulas and needles inserted by my trembling hands, or by inept nurses and careless or inexperienced registrars.

A lump rises to my throat from somewhere deep inside. He wants to live so much and has fought hard, valiantly. But I am exhausted, defeated by a multitude of traumas, having been forced to witness his immense suffering, and suffering with him, for him. I am exhausted by the rollercoaster ride of hope and horror. For years I have stood by him, protected him, advocated on his behalf, cared for him, and striven to do it all with as much grace as I could muster. Who would have thought I could ever be ready for him to die? But now, he has no quality of life and I'm no longer prepared to 'do this together,' as I swore I would at the beginning of his illness. The recent and sudden deterioration of his health has ripped away the last shreds of his dignity. All the falls, the blood, the accidents in bed, the nappies, and worse. I cringe for his lost dignity; I cannot take it anymore. He has always been such a neat, proud, and private man.

Viggo hears my footsteps as I enter the room. He turns his head ever so slowly, communicating with his eyes before mouthing something very softly. I feign a cheerful face, as if no one is dying here, and walk over to his bed, bending gently over his prone frame.

'What did you say, Treasure?'

'I said, "Mimi, is it really you?"'

'What do you mean?'

'That's what I said the first time we made love, up at your apartment. Remember?'

'Yes, I do.'

Reassured, he shuts his eyes and his face becomes peaceful. Busy sounds reach us from the nurses' station outside his palliative care room. I stroke his head. His hair is quite thin now, but still dark for a man turning 70. I wonder how much longer I will be able to share a space with him, or touch him, or tell him that I love him.

I watch the cover on the bed move slowly up and down with each of his breaths and think about the first time we made love.

CHAPTER 2

The affair began the moment I reached for the phone book to search for his number in the summer of 1975, the day after we—my husband Michael, our two small daughters Cassandra and Rebecca and I—arrived at my father's place in Copenhagen. We had seen a counsellor before we left who advised us to take a family holiday in order to repair our seven-year marriage following years of Michael studying during the day and working at night. I had agreed to take this trip but in truth, homesickness for Denmark and my family was more of an incentive than my recently diminished investment in the relationship.

It hadn't always been like this, of course. Ever since I'd given up on my plan to study medicine, my alternative purpose was to be a good wife and mother. Being a divorce child myself, the last thing I wanted was for my marriage to end, and I had adored Michael and been proud of him. He was the authority I would quote to others whenever my opinions (which were really his) were disputed. I did everything for him. Typed his essays, ironed his shirts, washed, cooked, shopped, and parented our toddlers on my own. Tried to make ends meet on his meagre and changeable income, which depended more on how long he felt like driving during his taxi shifts than on the financial needs of our family. I would fly out of bed at night to prevent crying toddlers from waking him, staggering like a drunk from sleep deprivation. I'd attempt to keep our little ones quiet each day until he emerged from his undisturbed sleep to shower, and then leave again—but not before first disputing some part of my parenting in front of the children, who would then cry for him and become unmanageable.

With Michael largely absent from the family, I had been locked in the house alone with small children for over four years. His frequent challenges to my parenting values eventually tipped me over the edge one night, when I suddenly became confused—was it or wasn't it important to teach my children to eat with a knife and fork? Michael thought it unnecessary. I sought counselling, and it was not a day too early, as I often lost control of my anger with my babies. I hated myself for having become the parent I had never wanted to be, and sobbed at the realisation that I had completely failed as a mother.

During counselling, it emerged that I had felt trapped in a situation that was too similar to my own early childhood isolation. As a small child, I was not allowed out of our tiny flat because my parents feared the fascists who were still around after the Second World War. My mother's ability to love had been largely extinguished in Auschwitz, where her crime, stated on her German prisoner index card, was that she was Jewish. Her unspoken injunction was that I must not have any needs, not demand warm emotions, and certainly not show that I needed her.

I had married early with the twin purposes of getting away from home and creating the family I'd never had. Now it seemed that I had not only failed as a mother, but that the problem was the marriage itself. My failed parenting was at least partly the result of Michael's obstructiveness and lack of emotional, physical, and adequate financial support.

After this revelation, I could no longer prevent Michael's fall from the elevated position I had afforded him. It was immediate, and similarly steep. I couldn't un-see the damage he had caused us, or turn a blind eye to the many incidents I had previous suppressed and that now came flooding back to me, each a potential nail in the coffin of our relationship.

Like the time when our youngest was in hospital with suspected cystic fibrosis and I had been going out of my mind with worry (a regular characteristic of holocaust survivor children, always expecting a catastrophe rather than a more benign possibility). When I tried to share my concern, Michael told me he had to study, so could I please talk to someone else about it! Then there was his unpredictable moodiness; his self-importance and preciousness; and more. The realisation that my marriage might be the problem rather than any innate evilness or flaw on my part had immediate effects. My self-esteem, confidence, and parenting quickly improved with the counselling, in equal proportion to my diminishing admiration of Michael.

By and by, I began fantasising about other men, a sexual reawakening that was sudden and unexpected. Before we left Australia, I thought of *him*—Viggo, whom I had met as a schoolgirl—and what might have been, how it would have felt. One night or maybe over a period of many nights, my desire for him grew until I knew somewhere inside that when I returned to Denmark, I had to see him.

Now, as I sat in my father's armchair and leafed through the phone book on that Copenhagen morning, I didn't know what to expect. I thought maybe he was dead. Maybe he really had carried out his threat to suicide when I left for Australia to marry Michael.

Or maybe he still lived at home with his mother. But more likely, he was married and had a house full of children. My initial intention, I told myself, was to look up the phone numbers of my old friends and reconnect with them. But somehow the phone book opened on *K*, fell right open on the first letter of his surname. My hands shook as I quickly scanned up one page, down another.

And suddenly, there it was. This was not a common Danish name, so it had to be him. The listing said he was an architect. I was very surprised, very excited—an architect! I had often watched my father's architect friend designing, and was fascinated by his creative ability. Viggo, an architect! Michael had only just finished studying and was earning a meagre living as a taxi driver at night.

I had clearly underestimated Viggo, had never imagined that he had it in him to join such a noble profession!

But who was this 'Gilla' beside his name? Was it a business partner? Or maybe he shared his place with his sister. Wasn't his sister called Gilla? Or—could it be his wife? I dialled the number. No one picked up the phone. All that day I tried to call. At first, I was disappointed, but later I began to panic, wondering whether he had perhaps gone away on a prolonged holiday, or changed his phone number. In that case I might not get to see him while I was in Denmark.

In the end, I settled for his mother's old phone number, took a deep breath, and recklessly made the call. 'Thirty-two thirty-six,' came her voice, repeating the number I had dialled. Yes, that must be Viola. She sounded just as she had years ago. She was surprised, almost shocked, when she heard it was me. I tried to sound worldly, telling her about my little family and the last eight years, all in a few hurried sentences. Then I asked about him, casually. She said she thought that maybe it would be better if he called me, or then again, he might decide not to. She would get in touch with him and tell him I was in Copenhagen. His wife was very jealous, so maybe it was best if he didn't contact me. But she would leave it up to him.

So, he *was* married ...

All weekend, I walked around the phone like a lioness, ready to grab it in case he called. But no call came. Finally, the phone rang on Monday morning. I knew it would be him. I sat down comfortably with my cigarettes at the ready before picking up the receiver.

'Hello? This is Viggo, May I speak to Mimi?'

I joked in a slightly put-on voice, 'I'm sorry, but she isn't here at the moment.'

'Oh.'

There was a disappointed silence. Why did I feel hot and cold all over, why was I grasping the phone so hard, why was my hand so slippery and clammy on the receiver? Why couldn't I speak properly, why, oh why, did I feel like crying? I couldn't even get out a lighthearted laugh, only a flat, 'Okay, it *is* me.'

'Oh, I thought I recognised your voice.'

'Hi. How are you?'

'Very well, and you? My mother told me you have two little girls?'

'Yes, one is two and a half; the other one is four and a half. They're very lively, not like Danish children.'

'And what have you been doing all these years?'

'Making children. It's fun trying, you know! Your mother told me that you've just finished your degree and how well you've done. Congratulations! How come you became an architect?'

'Well, actually it was my wife who talked me into it. I'm glad she did.'

'Your wife ... do you have any children?'

'No, none.'

'Why? How long have you been married?'

'Five years ... you know, it's strange, but I've been thinking about you constantly for the past two weeks. When my mother called me and said, "Guess which old flame of yours is in town?" I didn't even hesitate to say your name. I had this feeling about you, I wanted to call your father and ask how you were getting along. Isn't it strange?'

'Have I bewitched you?' I said, followed by a throaty laugh.

'You did that a long time ago,' he answered softly.

'Well, I've been thinking about *you* a lot lately too, since I knew we were coming. Maybe we have an invisible link?'

'Mimi, I've been sick. I finished my degree in five years instead of six, and the last two weeks before the exam I didn't sleep at all. Then I had a breakdown and was hospitalised for four months. I thought I was Jesus, and I wanted to be Jewish. I talked a lot about you, even to my wife.'

'I'm sorry to hear you've been unwell. Are you better now?'

'Thanks. I'm feeling better every day.'

'So your wife knows about me?'

'I told her about you when we first met.'

'Would you like to see me?'

'Yes, when?'

'I don't look the way I used to. I've become old and haggard and wrinkled and tired.'

He laughed. 'Old?' You're only twenty-six, and anyway, I haven't become younger.'

'Have you still got your Beatles haircut?'

'Yes, and now I have a moustache as well.'

'A moustache? Oh, well ...'

'Can we meet alone this first time? I'd like to see your children, but I'd rather see you alone first.'

'How about my husband, would you like to meet him?'

'No, what do I have in common with your husband!'

His voice changed to that pouty, cranky sound of the loser I knew so well from many years before.

'All right, I will meet you at Hellerup station in the waiting room. What time suits you?'

'I'm still only working half days during my recovery, and I always have lunch at 12. Shall we say 1 o'clock?

'Yes, okay. Do you have a car?'

'Not at the moment. I'm picking it up tomorrow night. It's in for repairs. Shall we say tomorrow then?'

'All right, see you tomorrow. Goodbye.'

'Goodbye.'

I put the phone down and my children were suddenly all over me, but I hardly noticed them. Why had I needed to suppress a sob when I heard his voice? Why had I almost burst out crying when he asked me how I had been? How *had* I been? It would be strange to meet him the following day. I felt butterflies in my stomach. Well, I thought, I didn't love him when I returned to Australia to marry Michael, but I'd still feel strange meeting him again.

I was excited. I decided not to tell my husband. It would seem odd to ask him to mind the children while I went to meet up with an old boyfriend. So instead, I told him that I wanted to go to the city by myself. That was quite acceptable to him. He had suggested that I go out as often as I liked, to make up for having been alone with the children for years while he studied and worked.

I knew that something would happen as soon as I saw Viggo again. No, I knew it would happen even before I saw him.

I took care to dress well, and arrived on time for the meeting. He wasn't there. I walked around the waiting room, then realised that he might be watching my impatience from afar and decided to stand still outside the bookshop, looking blankly at the display. Then suddenly he was by my side, looking sideways at me. He shook his head, shook it again, and whispered, 'Mimi,' as if he hadn't believed it *would* be me until he saw me.

I looked back at him. He had changed—so much. His face was thin and drawn, accentuated by a drooping moustache. We started walking, and kept on walking, ending up near the water at a lookout at the end of a quiet residential street.

I sat down on a low railing, dangling my legs. The water was chopping gently just beneath me. He sat down next to me. There we were, like two shipwrecks washed up on the shore. I, much too thin, burnt out, riddled with guilt about my bad parenting, disillusioned. He, still in negotiation with his parched and tortured soul about the nature of reality. We had no right to be there, no right to talk, we were a world apart. He had a wife and I had a husband and two little girls. A world apart, living on opposite sides of the earth. We didn't know each other anymore. We didn't know what each of us had become in the intervening years since we had last seen each other. I stole a glance at his profile every few minutes. For some reason, we didn't dare look into each other's eyes. It seemed much too dangerous.

A man was trimming his hedge nearby. A lawnmower was busily humming in one of the gardens. Viggo said with a smile as he looked at the man, 'I like gardening, messing around, trimming hedges, mowing lawns.' The man curiously observed us, strangers he hadn't seen hereabouts before.

'Oh, you mean making sure the grass won't ever grow past a crewcut?' I cut in with mild sarcasm, disappointed that he was such a bore.

'Yes, I think it would be nice to use my Sundays in that way,' he said, ignoring my remark.

Nodding in the direction of the man nearby, I asked, 'Do you think he's happy? Don't you think it's a good way to get a heart attack, after some clout walks on your precious flowerbeds?'

'No, maybe you're right, maybe they aren't happy. Maybe I wasn't happy either, at the state hospital where I was recuperating. But I thought I liked pottering around, gardening. At the time I thought it was lovely.'

I fell silent.

He talked about how he had just recovered from his nervous breakdown. He had been diagnosed with bipolar disorder. I tried to remember the psychology essays I had typed for Michael. It didn't surprise me; Viggo had always been rather sad and thoughtful. He told me how he had loved being 'mad'. He hadn't wanted to recover. His saying that made me think that maybe he hadn't had a good reason to recover. Maybe ... He also told me that a lot of things about me had come out while he was sick. At a time like that, he said, all the garbage of the soul comes pouring forth. His wife had heard all of it.

In turn, I told him that my husband and I weren't on the best terms, that I couldn't cope with the children, that the whole family was wrong, somehow.

He said he and his wife had a lot in common, that she was a good woman. Then he blurted out, 'I've been thinking about you and dreaming about you every day for eight years. When I'm together with my wife I often imagine it's you, it could have been you ...'

I sat in silence for a while, absorbing his words. Oh, my God, I hadn't realised the extent of his feelings for me. Years before, he had written asking me whether I was sure I wanted to stay married to

Michael, because he had met a girl. I'd never responded. I had been happy with Michael and viewed Viggo's letters as intrusive and somewhat pathetic. Now, I was thinking that perhaps I shouldn't have looked him up. Perhaps he was still too unwell. This could all end very badly.

Nevertheless, I recklessly persevered, 'Do you remember the night we met?'

'Yes,' he answered. His eyes had a faraway pained look, revealing years of pent-up longing.

*

When we met on that November night in 1964, the first things I noticed about Viggo were his velvet-brown eyes, dark-brown Beatle cut, grey pants, pink shirt, black leather tie, and his open black leather waistcoat. I remembered the feeling of deep disappointment when he left the venue with his friends until one of my friends exclaimed, 'MIMI! Look down, look down!' We were standing at the window upstairs in the venue and there they were, on the opposite side of the street in the doorway of a shop, he between his two taller friends who were chiding him, pushing him sideways. He was tottering, laughing, looking up at me.

I was excited, partly from relief that he hadn't left, partly from fear. What would he do to me, why was he waiting? I was scared that they would leave, and I feared that they might stay. They were beckoning for me to go down. I just shook my head but kept looking down at them, looking at him. It was a good opportunity to look him over, to try to fathom what he was like. They didn't look tough at all, they looked like nice kids. Maybe I shouldn't be scared. Finally, the lights in the venue flicked off and on to indicate that it was closing time. We got up to leave. My legs were shaking so much I thought I would be unable to walk casually, as I intended. We got downstairs and I was a little frightened; I tried not to look back. He didn't come after us as we walked away. Again, I felt disappointed.

Then my friend Annette, whose 15th birthday we had just celebrated, called out, 'Look, he's coming!'

I looked back and saw him running towards us, his hair flying back, flapping up and down with each stride, the sides of his jacket flying open, his eyes very shy, yet forcing their gaze into mine; searching. He slowed to a walk beside me and saw me home to my friend's place where I was staying that night. There, we talked about ourselves. It was a strange sort of meeting. We knew nothing about each other, yet we longed to find out more. He admitted that he was already going steady with a girl. It was very late by the time he left. He saw me to the door and leant in and kissed me on the doorstep. The kiss seemed to go on forever, consuming me, soft and tender. His hands were on my shoulders. His breath was heaving and he let out a soft moan. I had never been kissed like that before. We parted shyly. The bulb on the stairway was blinking sleepily; there was a musty smell of damp wooden stairs mingled with the scent of his soap, his hair, his mouth. I hoped I would see him again. I hoped he would break up with his girlfriend.

'See you on Friday,' he whispered, and first the grey pants, then the dark jacket, and finally his flopping dark hair disappeared down the stairs.

*

'Yes, I remember how we met,' he said again, turning his glance back in my direction.

'And the night we slept together after I visited from Australia? I was 18 and you were 19, do you remember?'

'Yes, it was so lovely, just as I had imagined it would be like with you.'

We walked back through the suburban streets, the way we had come. It seemed so strange to walk next to each other. He had a shoulder bag hanging on his left shoulder, and my cigarettes and a box of matches were in my right hand. I slipped my free hand into his, and he squeezed mine in return. His hand was so soft. It felt right, like it always had.

'It feels nice,' I whispered.

'That's what I always tried to tell you,' he answered.

And then our eyes met, and I drowned in a pool of dark velvet brown.

'I had always imagined that you were happy,' he said. 'You just had to be. That was my only consolation, that one of us was really happy. It pains me that it didn't turn out that way. It's such a waste ... but you have two lovely little girls!'

'Yes, I know. And they *are* lovely. You must see them. They have curly hair like mine, poor kids, but it looks gorgeous on *their* little heads. They are so lively, so naughty—they are adorable. I'm just a bit burnt out; I've been with them too much on my own. But you must see them. You'd love them.'

'I'm sure I would. I'd love to see them.'

'How is it that you haven't any children? You used to love kids.'

'We decided not to have any. We want to travel, and children tie you down. My wife doesn't want any children and she might be getting too old. She's six years older than me. I don't want to have children with her anyway. The thought frightens me. I only ever wanted to have children with one girl. And that girl was you.'

By the time we got back to the station, we had almost agreed not to meet again. Or rather, I had said it would be better not to. Not after those kisses. It was so crazy. Yet sitting on a bench in front of the station, facing a busy street, I drew close to his face on an impulse, those soft lips of his like a magnet, and suddenly we were sharing something new, although it was something we already knew. Something that had nothing to do with the circumstances of my life, or his. Traffic was passing, a few horns were beeping, a mother walked past with a baby in a stroller and an older child who dragged his feet in tired pursuit. I felt a pang of guilt when I saw the mother's face, so gentle, the worry lines prominent, her eyes meeting mine and then looking past me, filing us away amongst lovers just as she had once been, as if it no longer mattered. The result was her situation. It was also mine, but there I was, heaving from kisses, my own children at home with their dad, expecting me back from my 'trip to the city'.

I recoiled; all I could think of was getting home. What was I doing here? I'd been through all this. My life had fallen into the very same neat patterns as had the woman's on the street. That time was over. I was her age, not some kind of wild teenager anymore …

'Will I see you again?' he asked.

I said I didn't know whether it was a good idea, but he could call some night around 9 if he wanted to. By then, I might have made up my mind whether to introduce him to my children.

As I walked home, I tried to rid myself of that heavy feeling of guilt. Yet at the same time, I was drunk on the craze of the Danish summer, the memory of his lips, the excitement stirring my body to new life. And I needed a new life. I felt I had died inside, that I was just the hollow shell of my old self, that I wasn't even real anymore, that I was just going through the motions. The soul had been missing from my life. But now it was beating inside me like a hammer, it wanted to live! It had discovered a glimpse of life, remembered that there *was* such a thing, after all ...

The fruit trees in the gardens I passed were heavy with ripening apples, pears, plums. Even the weeds contributed a sharp little smell. An unclipped branch from a hedge reached out to me. I just had to pull off a leaf and squash and roll it around between my fingers, then pull off its veins and smell my fingers that were saturated with the strong green sap of the leaf, like I used to do as a child. It was mid-summer. This was the Denmark I had so missed when I was 18.

The concrete footpath echoed under my feet, stirring up nature and life and this suburb, announcing me, the woman.

How could one help yearning at a time like this, how could one help being in love with life itself? My heart was pushing at my breast, my chest rising proudly, my feet hardly feeling the steps I took, the houses flying past my sharpened awareness. I didn't even know how I had walked this far.

His eyes danced in the soft summer air in front of me, the breeze embraced my face, touched my lips ... like he had touched them. I lifted a finger to my bottom lip, almost not daring to touch where he had kissed me with his lovely lips, so strange against mine. So strange, and yet so familiar. I had known how it would feel but the reality of it, living the dream, his warmth against mine, had been a shock.

Could I do this? Me? Was I still attractive, still desirable, and still special for him? My wonder was paralleled by the pleasure, the memory of his kiss jangling my nerves. I could hardly wait to see what happened next, I hardly dared hope we might meet again. How could I control the feelings that he had awakened in me? Would I even want to control them? No. Oh no ...

As I walked back to my father's place, feeling a million things, my senses open to everything around me, I realised that I would see him again if he called. If only he called!

Back at the apartment I felt a sense of separateness, as if I somehow no longer belonged. I looked at my husband. He looked like a familiar stranger, or a distant family member. The children hardly noticed me arrive, running past me as they played.

I thought, yes, I will see him again. Maybe he will look different next time, not quite so drawn. Maybe I will, too, from pure expectation.

CHAPTER 3

I catch up with Doctor Death in the corridor and ask him in a low voice about Viggo's current prognosis. He answers in the usual way: it could be days, or weeks, or perhaps even months. During the conversation, he comments that it is a shame Viggo is still so lucid, because the dying process is much harder for him.

I have no doubt that it is due to his razor-sharp intelligence and wilfulness; he never gives in. After his strokes, he doggedly remembered the three test items the doctors initially asked him to memorise, reciting them back to them on their daily rounds for days afterwards, even when they didn't ask. Yet it was quite obvious, by his general confused behaviour and increased anxiety, that his brain had been damaged.

He specifically had trouble with online banking and recalling his password. He was therefore denied access, which disempowered and frustrated him and caused him endless concern.

Back in his room I see that he is asleep. I slow my steps and walk quietly to the chair. I sit beside the bed and steal a glance at his face, trying to look at him as objectively as a stranger might. Oh, my God, his face! The skin is yellowish and taut over his ears and high cheekbones; his cheeks are hollow. His eyes, his lovely eyes, have receded into dark cavities. Those lips that used to be full and sensual are now much thinner, his mouth much smaller. His arms and legs, hidden below the sheet, are mere skin and bone. The last time Nicola visited and massaged his feet, I noticed with horror that even the soles of his feet have started to curl up, hollowing inwards, drying up.

I stand to adjust his pillow gently and sit back, waiting, waiting, letting my mind wander back to a much younger and healthier Viggo.

*

The phone rang at exactly 9 o'clock. I jumped and picked up the receiver. My heart was racing, my hands shaking.

'Hello?'

'Hi, it's me. Can I see you again?'

'Yes.'

From the time I was a child, I had acquired the ability to suspend empathy, and my seductive nature must have left a trail of misery behind me as I grew into a young woman: my stepbrother, Gabi, who had joined us in Denmark but was banished back to Hungary when I was 14 after an illicit, but essentially innocent, flirtation with me; a blur of boys and men, one after another. I had mastered the knack of inviting intimacy while skilfully avoiding vulnerability, and had mostly remained in control of relationships, including within my marriage. I had fallen in love, had loved, but never enough to let any man entirely under my skin.

But now, as I was making plans to meet Viggo again, I instinctively felt that this was about to change. It seemed significant when I said 'yes', even dangerous. It was as if I had just agreed to enter a body of water that was much too deep for me. I could get hurt, the same as I had hurt Pista long ago.

Pista was the first boy I had kissed, at the age of 13. A year later he committed suicide, and I was at least partly the cause of his fatal decision. I got to know Pista shortly after we both arrived in Denmark. He was two years my senior, so he must have been nine at the time. Our parents had become friends in the refugee camp and kept in touch. Pista's father repaired shoes and his mother worked as a cleaner at a pharmacy. She was hard of hearing, wore a hearing aid, and her husband often let it be known that he thought her less than bright. Listening to him talk about her in that way made me uncomfortable as a child, as if I was forced to be complicit in her humiliation. Our families often spent Saturdays or Sundays in one another's company. The adults would invariably play cards. Pista and I were left to our own devices and soon discovered that we had something very specific in common: we were both abused—me, physically (not sexually) by my stepfather, and Pista, emotionally, by his father. Pista confided that he was forced to be the Danish translator for his parents, and his father was demanding and scathing, often putting him down and calling him an idiot, although Pista was actually very smart. My stepfather, who had seen the earth moving on top of mass graves in a concentration camp during World War II —because of those buried alive—and experienced German boots on his emaciated body, intermittently hit me with blows that would leave me gasping for breath. I never knew why he did it.

I don't remember exactly when Pista and I first started talking about paying them back by committing suicide but over the years, we embellished on this fantasy and imagined with glee how sorry our parents would be. Then Pista's voice broke, and his new hee-haw laughter annoyed his dad, who often told him to stop laughing and shut up. I didn't understand this; I loved his laughter. In fact, I loved him exactly as he was, with his wispy dark hair, the scent of his special cologne, and his dark-brown eyes.

Inevitably, we started to talk about what it would be like to kiss and began planning for the auspicious event. By that time, we were corresponding in between our family get-togethers and exchanging love letters. Finally, we decided that we would kiss the next time we met. But how to start, and where would it be safe away from adult eyes? We looked around my room and thought we could meet behind the door in case someone came in suddenly. We settled on a time after lunch. We were both very tense, but when the time arrived, we met in the corner of the room behind the door. I still remember the shock of how unexpectedly warm his lips felt on mine, followed by the shock of running out of breath and frantically trying to work out how to breathe and kiss at the same time. Then it was over, and I was very shy and in emotional turmoil at the feelings the kiss aroused in me. Part of me wanted more, but another part felt disgust, as if what I had done was dangerous and wrong.

Sometimes I thought I never wanted to see Pista again, and after the kiss his letters became more frequent and fervent. They sounded very adult-like, ardent and urgent, and each letter contained passionate

Hungarian love poems in his hand, although I later found out that they were copied from the writings of a published poet. As a 13 or 14-year-old, I felt very uncomfortable with that level of attention.

Around the same time, I commenced dance classes on weekday afternoons, and my dance partner was a lovely boy who soon began cycling over to my apartment building after school. I would meet him downstairs and we would go for walks and bicycle rides together. Now more than ever I wanted to distance myself from Pista and the emotional responsibility he had placed upon me. I thought of a terrible scheme: I was pining for the new lip balms that came in a variety of flavours. They were newly on the market and sold at pharmacies. To my eternal shame, I, who prided myself on my honesty and ethics, wrote to Pista that he should ask his mother to steal one of each lip balm for me, or it would be the end of our relationship. Fortunately, given my cooling feelings for Pista, we did not see his family for a while, and then one morning before school, a letter arrived from him. It was a goodbye letter. He wrote that by the time I received it, he would be dead. He wrote that I knew the reason why. He wrote that he wanted me to have his most precious possession, a camera. I must have run in to tell my mother and stepfather in a panic, because they said I should go to school and they would look into it. I will never forget the dread

I felt as I was sitting at my desk and the door opened slightly, my stepfather and the principal entering the class, motioning for me to go outside with them. My stepfather looked emotional. I knew then that Pista had died.

I was inconsolable, and could not understand that he was no more. I wondered whether it was my threat of breaking up with him that had tipped him over the edge. I dropped lilies of the valley flowers on his coffin at his funeral, and went home to pen a story about him, trying to relieve some of my turmoil and grief. Sometime later, his parents came for a visit, and I learnt that he had written three letters: one to his school, one to me, and one to his parents. His grades at school had declined and he had forged his father's signature on the last school report and taken it back to school without showing it to his parents. On the day he died, he had timed the execution of his suicide to coincide with the exact time his mother normally came home from work. He had gone into the kitchen, closed the kitchen door and turned on the gas oven. He had written clear instructions to his mother about how she should save him, including that she should turn off the gas and call the ambulance. But she had decided to go shopping that day. He was found slumped at the kitchen door, having obviously attempted to get out when he realised that she was late. He had just wanted to frighten them into being kind to him, perhaps because of his grades.

Then the parents handed me a bag with Pista's camera and lots of lip balm tubes in all different flavours. I could have sunk through the floor in shame when I saw the lip balms, which his mother would have stolen for him. It did nothing to reassure me that my threat to break up with him had not played a major part in his suicide. He had written that I would understand the reason, and I knew he was referring to our many conversations about his desire to avenge his father's emotional abuse. But we had never talked about a plan, and I wondered how he had worked out what to do. Receiving my 'ransom' made me almost certain that he had questioned my love for him when faced with the thought of losing me for a bunch of lip balm tubes; it would have contributed to his despair.

Pista's death was a terrible loss and it scarred me for life. I still remember his birthday every year and think about how old he would have been and the life he might have led, how many children he might have had. I also felt very sorry for his parents. He was their only child. But at the time, despite my grief, it was a relief to know that I did not owe him my love anymore. More than two decades later, I decided to rid myself of all the love letters I'd ever received, Pista's amongst them. I sat on the floor sobbing and read each one of his letters, when, inexplicably, I found the room bathed in the scent of his cologne, a scent I had completely forgotten.

*

'When is best for you?' Viggo now asked.

'Oh, it doesn't matter, any day really, as long as it's during the day.'

'I can't any other time anyway. I always have lunch at 12, so how about 1 o'clock again?'

'That suits me too. I'll bring the baby this time. She'll be all right without a nap, I guess.'

'I'll see you the day after tomorrow then.'

'Okay.'

I told my husband that I had been in contact with Viggo and planned to go out that day with him. I said I'd like him to meet our children one at a time, as it would be more manageable than taking both. The two men had known about each other for years, and Michael didn't seem to mind and even said he wanted to meet Viggo, confident of my loyalty. After all, both of us knew there had been many times in our relationship that I should have left him but had stayed.

It was very hot and I couldn't find my bikini bottoms anywhere, so I just wore my undies. Viggo would probably want to go to the beach; there wasn't anything else worth doing in Denmark on such a rare sunny day. I dressed my toddler up in a pretty dress and at 1 o'clock exactly, Viggo rang the buzzer downstairs. As I passed the mirror in the hallway, I thought my face looked relaxed and excited. I was looking forward to this outing. It was a long time since I had looked forward to anything, I thought, as I slowed my pace to walk my toddler down the unfamiliar stairs in my father's apartment building.

When we reached the street and I caught sight of him, my heart started to race crazily. I told him he looked really good, and he answered that it was probably the anticipation of seeing me. He was holding the door of his Mini Moke open for us, glancing at my baby next to me. I felt very shy. He had never seen me in the role of mother, and I didn't feel like the mother I had been just a few days before. I seemed too independent, too unattached, to be a mother. It was a strain to be the old me, and I didn't yet know who the new one was.

We got in the car and as I expected, headed for the beach. The baby had to lie down in the back as the car was only licensed for two adults. He chose to go to a beach that was quite a distance away. He was concentrating on the road, the car flying past blocks of flats, then houses, then fields. He looked very sunburnt, very determined, very relaxed. I wondered just how much I meant to him, how much it meant to him that I was sitting at his side and that we were going to the beach together, with my child. It was hot, and both the baby and I were perspiring.

Again I felt unusually alive, my senses fully awake. I noticed the stones on the ground; tough dune grass emerging from sandbanks; how sand from previous stormy days had swept around the trunks of the tough, dry pine trees. Our feet were bare, burning on the sand underfoot, the pine needles piercing the soles of our feet. The scents of hot sweet pine, hot dry sand, rotting seaweed, salt.

We walked gingerly and it was a relief to spread out the towel on the flat greyish-white sand and sit down. Tiny pebbles under the towel made small bulges. I picked them out from beneath the towel and offered them to my little girl to play with and to throw into the ocean. I took off my t-shirt, revealing my bikini top, and felt very shy. He had seen me eight years previously when the skin on my stomach was taut, when my breasts were firm. My body had withered somewhat since then. The skin on my stomach was a little wrinkled after the children, there was a stretch mark, and my navel looked a bit battered. I kept on my jeans as I only had panties underneath. He teased me to take them off, peeking inside and saying that my panties were cute, that I could easily wear them instead of bikini bottoms. But I didn't want to, a shy me emerged, an innocent person, innocent to him, to us, an unexplored new me.

My every word, every move, was unprecedented. The way I held my head, glances, gestures ... they were no longer natural. I was excruciatingly self-conscious.

He looked at me approvingly, his eyes teasing. He lay on his stomach and I saw his powerful wide back, the shoulder-blades broad with dormant strength. His body could command me. I was lying there, leaning back on my elbows, outwardly seemingly unaware, but his body was speaking to mine. We were several feet apart, talking or lying quietly and listening to the lazily chopping waves, the hum of radios and a quiet conversation in the distance, my little girl's blabber, the thud of the pebbles she was throwing into the sand. Through all this I was agonisingly aware of his body. My eyes were glued to his lips whenever he spoke. His lips weren't saying what he was saying; they beckoned me, his teeth biting down on his bottom lip as he laughed. His eyes weren't meeting mine either; his gaze was on my lips. Unconsciously, I licked my lips with my tongue even though they weren't dry. I was lying there on the towel, every fibre of my body pulsating and alive.

My little girl kept asking to go to the toilet and was about to squat, which immediately embarrassed him. There was a toilet way down where the car was parked. In the meantime, she became more daring, moving away from us, throwing the stones into the water, letting the little waves lick her tiny toes. Viggo leapt up and went to play with her in the water for a while and she laughed big, giggling, joyful laughs. As I watched, I was trying to understand why it felt so right, yet why it was so wrong. He came back and for a while, for fun, we talked about how she could really have been ours, whether she would have looked much different, how a child of ours might have looked. As she came back to fetch more stones, he looked searchingly at her features. His eyes were dark, almost black, and somehow inward-looking. I asked him what he was thinking, while moving my elbow a little closer to his arm, my fingers yearning to touch his skin. There was such electricity between us. He must have felt it too.

He watched the curly-headed toddler approach the waves once more, then he moved over quickly and covered my lips with his. The combination of the beachy smells, the sun baking our bodies, the sand, and the kiss made me hot with desire. Slowly, our lips parted. Slowly, our eyes opened into the depth of the other's and lingered; words were choked back. I didn't understand what was happening to me. But I couldn't let it happen.

Keeping a nervous eye on my little one, I wavered between thinking I had to have him, but that I mustn't. It felt as if I wasn't even living in my world anymore. My only goal in life narrowed to being embraced by those strong, olive-tanned arms, the skin taut and shiny; my body yearned to be caressed by his soft fingertips, to be possessed and taken by his body. All the while, his body was seemingly unaware and my face revealed nothing. I kept holding his gaze, forcing his eyes to lock with mine, swimming senselessly into dark-brown velvet, sinking, sinking, into those depths. I seemed to see his very insides, to feel them, to *be* them. All the time, in my conscious mind, was my puzzlement at these feelings, my conscience telling me how wrong it was to feel this way, yet wanting to continue. I could not stop myself. I didn't want to; it no longer seemed necessary or important. It felt irresponsible and reckless, but I didn't care. It was a strange sensation, like being pulled by myself against my own will, letting go, watching myself disappear in the distance with arms stretched out towards the promise of unadulterated joy.

My little girl returned. She was thirsty, and I experienced the strange feeling of having to suddenly act normally. It was difficult to remember how to think practically, to hear my own voice speak English and sound so foreign, so matter-of-fact, practical, and parent-like, so alien to how I was feeling. I didn't sound like the person I had suddenly become; I should have sounded soft and caressing. We got up and walked to the ice-cream stand. I was walking awkwardly on the hot surface and the stones, feeling observed and trying to be someone Viggo might like without knowing what that would be. By then, it was too hot on the sand for the little one and I picked her up and carried her. Our bodies sweated against each other and she became heavier as we walked. I was soon out of breath. He tried to take her but she clung to me, refusing him.

I took her to the toilet and then bought her a drink. It was so strange. He had already bought himself a drink, and I then bought one for my little girl and me. It was a reminder that we were strangers and that we did not belong together. I hated him for that, so cold, such pettiness. There he sat, by himself in the shade on a beach drinking a soft drink. It looked so silly. I felt flushed from the heat and my own embarrassment at the whole situation. What were we doing here? We had nothing in common. Here was this sensible Protestant guy, a man who always did the right thing at the correct time, a smug man-boy, sipping his drink while I was tending to my little girl, demonstrably separate from us. I was unhappily married, and this scene somehow accentuated that *I* was the unhappy one. He was having fun. It was simply a lucky coincidence that he was still only working half days while I was in Denmark. He could continue to see me without hurting his wife—she wouldn't know. I suddenly felt very alone and insecure.

Soon after, we started out for home. The car was hot to the touch; the back of his shirt became dark with perspiration. I didn't try to talk with him, there seemed no point. I didn't really want to see him again. The little one had fallen asleep in the back by the time we were halfway. Just before we got back, I asked him if we could park somewhere. I don't know why; the devil was driving me. The baby was asleep in the back, it seemed an opportune time, his lips touched mine, his hand squeezed my leg, and then his hands were everywhere. I didn't push them away. I was surprised at that and at how my hands found their way to his neck, his chest, his stomach. I had an urgent need to lie down, and I was desperately thinking about where this might be possible but couldn't think of anywhere.

I thought about the next time we might meet. It would be a good thing to take my other child because I doubted whether I'd be able to control myself if we were alone.

We kissed again and each time our lips parted, we could hardly stand the pain of the parting. He whispered my name, gently drawing my face with the tip of a finger, his eyes staring at my forehead, beyond it, somehow, before meeting my gaze.

Then he sighed and started the engine.

CHAPTER 4

The next day at lunch, the phone rang while I was telling my husband that I had arranged to go out with Viggo again after we finished eating, this time taking our elder daughter with me. The call was probably from Viggo, cancelling our outing.

It *was* him.

'I'm downstairs. Didn't you hear me toot?'

'No, we were just eating. Come on upstairs, we haven't finished yet.'

'No, I don't want to, I don't want to meet your husband.'

'Oh, come on, he wants to meet *you*.'

'All right.'

'He's coming upstairs,' I told my husband. My heart was beating hard, and I knew that my face was flushed. Now I was running late, and the child had to have her lunch, necessitating this unplanned meeting. It was risky to have them meet, a bit like telling half-truths designed to make lies more difficult to detect.

I walked down the hallway to open the door for him. He was next to me in seconds, taking the steps three at a time, hair flopping, his eyes urgent and haunted.

'Mimi, I've got to talk with you,' he blurted out breathlessly.

I looked at him, surprised.

'Later, when we're in the car. Come on in.'

My husband shook hands with him. Viggo sat down at the table with us and waited. I offered him some lunch but he said he had already eaten. I told him in Danish to speak with my husband; he could speak English, couldn't he? They started up a conversation about economics and politics, looking at each other with approval, the situation wincingly horrible. I couldn't finish my food.

'Come on, or you'll be left behind,' I said, beckoning to my eldest child. She was very keen now that her baby sister had had a turn.

The men shook hands again, and we left. The atmosphere in the car was loaded; the child sensed something and was attention-seeking. I hadn't wanted to take her; I had wanted to be alone with him. I had only brought her along to protect myself, on the pretext that he should meet her, but we could have left her at home as he had already met her there.

'Isn't she beautiful?' I asked him in Danish.

'I liked the little one better. This one seems too spoiled.'

'She isn't, she's just very confused and unhappy. My husband allows her to do everything, and I react by being too strict. We're all unhappy.'

My daughter kept interrupting and whining from the back, louder and louder. She wouldn't let us talk, up to her usual unhappy tricks. We decided to drive to a park, hoping that maybe she would let us talk then, but it didn't work out that way. We found a little shop with a playground next to it. We all had a soft drink and when she finished, I sent her off to the playground. Viggo and I could only exchange a few sentences at a time before she called out or came back to us. She was very hostile and cold towards him. We couldn't help touching, and then she would rush up and we would quickly part in case she noticed. Nevertheless, she was aware of the atmosphere between us. It was heavy with longing and with us fighting against it. Hundreds of questions and past memories haunted us and were written in our glances. We didn't have to say anything, do anything. She would notice regardless.

This was not how she knew her mother, this was not the way Daddy and Mummy were together, this was a man that Mummy was meeting. It was not a lady friend, he wasn't nice like they were. He hardly noticed her and when he did, he just looked at her thoughtfully. I felt terribly uncomfortable with this little chaperone of mine and now knew that I had to see him alone.

As we walked back towards the car, she suddenly tucked her hand into his. He almost jumped. It was like an electric shock, he told me in Danish, looking down at her warmly. I held her other hand and the three of us walked together towards the car. Everyone would have thought we were a family. Our eyes met above her head. On the way home, the little grouch finally, blissfully, fell asleep in the back, and we parked.

'What did you want to talk to me about?'

'Look, Mimi, I've thought this over. I haven't slept all night. I love you; I can't go on like this. I'm going to ask my wife for a divorce. I want us to marry.'

'Whoa! What about me? I don't know how I feel about you. I don't even know if I love you. I want you, but I don't know if I feel anything else. It's true that Michael and I have problems, but splitting up was not part of the agenda. We're a family, and we have plans. I want my children to attend a particular alternative school. I've read a lot about it and that's what I want for my kids. And we're heading back to Sydney soon to find a permanent house to live in.

I've been looking forward to this, making us a lovely home. Besides, now that my husband has completed his honours degree, I've finally found my calling and want to study early childhood, to save children from the kind of terrible teachers I experienced as a child. We're only just about to start living our real lives.

Viggo wouldn't be dissuaded.

'Look, I have a friend, a client, actually. He wants me to redesign the guttering on his house, and he's thinking of renting it out. It has a nice back yard. And of course your children could attend whatever type of school here too. Oh, look, I'm just so desperately in love with you. I can't go on this way, with pretty visits, pretending to be friends. It's got to be now, Mimi. Make up your mind. I don't want to go on this way. I can't carry on like this behind my wife's back, pretending that everything is normal when it's not. I'm going to talk with her today. Even if you don't want to stay in Denmark with me, I cannot live with her anymore. I guess it's always been there. You've always haunted me, day and night. And now to see you again? No, it's too much. I can't go on feeling the way I do.'

Oh my God, I thought, is this part of his mental illness?

'Look, we've only met three times, and up until a few days ago we've had zero contact for eight years. How can I make up my mind in the space of a few days? And don't, oh for Heaven's sake, please don't talk about how we could do it. It makes me feel sick. I can just picture it all, it would be terrible, we weren't supposed to share this future together. My husband and I were. This is what he and I have been working for, suffering for. I can't just throw it all to the wind now.'

'Yeah, I know. It's the same with us. Gilla is still studying and she works, doing cleaning in the mornings. We had nothing until recently. Now we have a furnished apartment, this car …'

Viggo shuddered at the thought of splitting everything up.

'And I can't just take the children away from their father,' I said. 'He loves them too. I could take the little one, but I can't imagine having one of my little girls growing up 12,000 miles away from me. They need each other too. Let's stop talking about this, please,' I said, with a wild look.

The despair at the mere possibilities! The thought alone was too much; I'd rather never see him again. I looked at him and thought, 'Never?'

I longed for him even when we were together; we just had to have each other.

'I want to see you, alone,' I said.

'Oh, that part doesn't matter, at least not much. I want to *live* with you!'

'I've never wanted anyone else since I married. I've never even looked at another guy. I didn't think of myself as potentially sexual in relation to others. That's how unaware I've been of other men.'

'Nor I. I haven't been with other women either, or even entertained the thought.'

'Do you want me too?' I asked.

He brought his face close to mine and kissed me for a long time. I was very wet. He squeezed my breasts and thigh hard, as if my body were his, commanding my body. I *had* to see him alone. His body excited me, his shoulders and chest were broad and masculine, he had become a man. I could hide in his chest, cry against those shoulders. I remembered how he had held my forehead when I had been violently ill from drinking too much at my good-bye party eight years before. No one else would have done that. Yes, I could cry in his arms.

I drew away and looked into his velvet-brown eyes, searching, searching. His eyes were the vulnerable part of him, soft, desperate, yearning, while his body was a man's body. He was breathing very hard, very quickly, his shoulders heaving up and down.

'Come on,' I implored, 'say yes.'

'Yes,' he sighed. 'But can't you see …'

I pressed a finger against his lips, silencing him.

'Please, let's drop it for now. It's impossible. You can't ask me to desert my children for you. I couldn't leave my marriage because of another man. I could only do that if or when my marriage ended. I don't know where it's at yet. I must give it a go. I can't leave, not yet. I must first be sure that it cannot work. You have nothing to do with my marriage. They're two separate things. It's as if you and I are something separate altogether, another life.'

'Well, that *is* true, isn't it?' He looked down, troubled.

We drove back. My daughter woke up when we arrived, curls stuck with perspiration against the side of her face from resting against the vinyl on the bench seat. He saw us to the door. She ran ahead upstairs.

'I'm desperately in love with you, Mimi,' he whispered. 'When shall we meet again?'

I froze. What did he want from me? He was always demanding the impossible, just like eight years before. I had to get there by myself. He couldn't convince me. His feelings would not change mine. I looked at him and, in that moment, he looked pathetic to me.

'Are you sure you can cope, that you won't become sick again?' I asked him.

'I don't think I'll get sick again. Anyway, I have some tablets I can take if I feel I'm losing my grip on reality. I must go and talk this over with my sisters. Would you like to come with me?'

'No, you go alone.'

'Can I see you on Friday?'

'Yes.'

'What do you want to do?'

'Meet me at my apartment; we'll go to the woods or something.'

I gave him the address and a meaningful glance. He didn't even notice, on account of his despair.

'What time?'

His eyes were hanging on my face, not even seeing it, only seeing his shattered dream somewhere amongst my features.

'At 1 o'clock.'

'It's always like this with you. You cannot make up your mind and in the end ... it always ends the same way.'

'I can't help that. I don't want to hurt you. I really don't. This isn't a holiday fling for me. Understand that much, at least. But let me work it out. You can't hurry me. My family comes first, and you have nothing to do with that.'

'I know. Well, I'd better go.'

'Bye.'

I ran upstairs. What would my husband think, watching me lingering in the doorway with him? We hadn't looked very cheerful either. I put on a happy face.

'Well, how was it?' my husband greeted me, not quite meeting my eyes.

I looked at him. He, too, looked pathetic. I decided to tell him.

'He wants a divorce. He also wants me to ask for a divorce.'

'And?'

'Well, our marriage isn't too hot, is it? It hasn't been for a long time. That has nothing to do with him though. But I think I'm in love with him.'

'No wonder then that he didn't want to meet me. I should have known that he still loved you. Well, what do you want to do?'

'I want to go on trying with our marriage. We can't split now. Things are about to get easier for us. You've finished your honours degree and we're about to start on a new chapter. I want to give it a go, for the children's sake.'

*

My father had rented an apartment for our use while we were in Denmark, and although we slept there at night, we spent most of our time at his place. But this day was different. It was Friday and I had to do the washing at the apartment and then send my husband off with the children to my father's where I would join them later—and all that before 1 o'clock. I'd been waiting for this day. Four days had passed since I'd last seen Viggo. I had to fit in a bath sometime before he came because I wanted to be lovely. I knew, and he knew, that *this* would be the day. I noticed in the bathroom mirror that my eyes were shining, my cheeks a bit flushed, and my lips a breathless swollen red from anticipation. But none of this was for my husband. With him, I was dull and flat, distant and elusive, evading his eyes.

Miraculously, everything worked out. I walked the family to the bus, I waved to the children where they were sitting in the back, watching me become smaller with the distance, and I felt lousy. I also felt sorry for my husband. I had made up an excuse about the reason I was going to join them later, but he had to know. He looked so dejected, so lonely, so confused, as if he didn't want to leave me there, but I was firm that they had to go. As I watched the bus leave, I was already missing my little children. They were still practically babies. What kind of a mother was I? Could they tell that I was somehow not a *real* mother? But as the bus turned, I saw that they were waving while absentmindedly looking elsewhere—secure, noticing nothing.

I looked at my watch and started to run. It was 1 o'clock, he would be at the apartment, or maybe he had gone, thinking I had left, or forgotten. As I turned back into our street, I saw him getting out of the car and started to laugh breathlessly, trying to suppress a giggle rising up from deep in my chest. It was perfect, we'd made it, no one knew. I ran up to him, out of breath, and we looked at each other, reality setting in. Our clandestine meeting seemed all wrong. We stole upstairs. People hereabouts knew everything, knew everyone. Even the old lady downstairs had come up one day and complained that I was not wearing slippers and it disturbed her to hear me walk around in my shoes upstairs. I felt watched. We quickly went inside and locked the door. He wanted to kiss me, but I lit a cigarette.

'Stop smoking, I want to kiss you!'

'Wait a minute …'

'Mimi, we won't see each other again, it's all wrong. I told Gilla, and I don't think we ought to continue this. She said that one just can't end five years of marriage like this—and I think she's right. This won't lead anywhere.'

His words hurt like a knife in my heart. He sat down on the couch. I got down on my knees in front of him and squeezed him to my breast.

'Okay, you can't stand not seeing me while I'm here, so it's fine if that's what you want.'

The words were almost inaudible; a big lump in my throat muffled my words. My lips were quivering; the tears were running down my cheeks, my nose, hanging suspended on my chin. He wiped them away.

'Don't cry, Mimi. I cried all day yesterday, and all night. I didn't sleep. But this is no good. I've made up my mind, I can't leave my wife. I don't know whether I love her, but she loves me, she's very much in love with me. And what about your husband and the children? I saw you all sitting together and eating, and I now realise that we can't do this—to anyone. We can't make all these people unhappy, and we wouldn't be happy either, knowing what we have done to two families.'

I felt very weak. He was right. I didn't know if I loved him or not, whether this was just a fling, a holiday escape, although I knew it wouldn't have happened with anyone else. We just felt we had a right to each other, somehow. Looking back, it would have been equally crazy *not* to have looked him up, or kissed him that first day at Hellerup train station. I started to unbutton his shirt and put my hand on his bare chest. His body was hot, really hot and soft. I kissed him and he squeezed me up to his chest with a moan. My breasts were touching him. Then he threw a sideward glance at me in his characteristic shy way, getting up and taking my hand.

'Come on,' he said, starting to undress.

I didn't want to take all my clothes off. What if my husband decided to come back for something? And I felt very shy. We didn't talk while we undressed; we just had to do this. We had to have this, just this once, for the rest of our lives. It was almost a ritual, akin to something little boys did when they exchanged the blood from a scratch to become blood brethren.

He hovered above me, whispering, 'Mimi, is it really you?'

'Yes,' I whispered back. I could feel him pressing against me and then suddenly he was inside me for the first time. My first thought was, 'Now I'm unfaithful.' The pain was terrible, as was the pleasure. I had never felt lovemaking that way before. Until that moment, I had not known what it meant to really make love, but somehow, I had always known that it would be perfect with him.

Afterwards, we washed and dressed quietly. Then we drove to the woods. They were magnificent. The trees were so tall that the lightest green leaves seemed to touch the bluest part of the sky. We walked hand in hand. Time was running out, we only had a few minutes left to be together. We sat down on a log, playing with the grass beneath us. I looked at him, burning with desire. I *had* to have him again. I wanted to kiss him, but he drew back. I got up and pulled him with me further into the woods where we would be undisturbed. Then I sat on him and made love like I'd never done before. It was hot; the perspiration was dripping off him, off me; my smell and his and the wild grass smell; nature smells; bees humming; mosquitoes feasting on our damp bottoms and thighs. But we didn't care, nothing mattered just then. Then from somewhere far away I heard his cry. It was loud and for a moment I thought maybe someone would hear, but I didn't care. I wanted to go on, but he didn't. It was time to go, it was no use continuing, it would hurt everyone. It was too selfish, and maybe it wasn't even real love. He asked me not to look so sad, and left me there when I said I preferred to walk to the station.

How could I not look sad, how could I say goodbye to this kind of loving? He could teach me, make me do things no one had taught me before.

Somehow, I pulled myself together, found my way to the station, and caught a train to my father's place. I sat in the train, feeling damp inside my trousers. My cheeks were still flushed; my heart was still beating fast. I looked at the other passengers and wondered whether they would see my eyes shining. Could they? Wouldn't my husband see? I didn't care just then. Somehow, things that used to matter did not matter anymore.

CHAPTER 5

I had a lot to think about on the train. I had always believed that love, the really deep kind of love, lasts forever. I was willing to contemplate that it might change over time, but I didn't think it would ever die. And there was my dilemma, realising that I might believe in a romantic idea but reality could be very different.

I had always been convinced that I could never be unfaithful while married. I'd thought I was a one-man girl once I was committed. And I was wrong. I could see now how unpredictable human nature can be, or at least *my* human nature, capable of negating and abandoning beliefs, morals, logic, and decency in favour of a sudden fervent desire. On the other hand, maybe it was predictable and only the timing was unpredictable.

The last two years of my marriage to Michael had deteriorated to the point that it seemed unsalvageable. Michael criticised, shamed, mocked, and humiliated me in a thousand ways, but for a long time I was impervious to it. His nickname for me was 'birdbrain', but I'd never realised it could be perceived as anything other than a loving term. He treated lovemaking similarly to our relationship—with disrespect. The first time I climaxed loudly, he burst out laughing. I was shocked and disappointed. After that, I had to choose either to disregard his reaction or alter mine. He often found it difficult to make love, and sometimes blamed this on something I had done. Inevitably, it all morphed into fulfilling his needs, which were only achieved when I lay quite still beneath him while he laboured above me. Added to that were a myriad of bad behaviours and thoughtless comments. All this crept up on me so that I hardly noticed the deterioration amidst the chaos of life with young children.

When I finally became aware of it, I told my husband what I felt, but he just shrugged it off. We hardly saw each other. I was with the children all day while he was out, studying and working. Slowly, I missed him less, my motivation to be with him decreased, and my own interests took over. I developed and grew away from him. Each time we were together, the wounds, the chasm, deepened, instead of healing. I felt it happening in the lonely nights, in the experiences of each day that we did not spend together, each time I witnessed our children's latest milestones on my own. I desperately tried to preserve the feelings I had held for him for so long, only to have them diminish despite myself and find myself fantasising about other men.

So it was understandable that I would be tempted to make love with Viggo. The real shock was to feel the emotions, to realise the contrast of what I had *not* felt for such a long time, my intense desire to keep on feeling, the dread of losing it and slowly dying again emotionally. I was shocked to realise that I was capable of loving someone else, that I could not resist it. I was shocked at the depth of my feelings and the crazy realisation that true feelings can never be known until properly tested.

It is difficult to hold on to love when one is separated. It requires the presence of the other person, the undeniable chemistry. As an 18-year-old sailing back to Australia to marry Michael after a separation of nine months, I could hardly recall what I felt for him, so I just had to trust in the past. My feelings for him returned instantly when I saw him there on the pier, searching the ship for my face amongst the crowd on the deck. I had taken a risk, but the difference between then and now was I had been free to do with my life what I wished, whereas now I was not. I thought back to just before our family holiday, to the nights when I had lain in bed thinking about men I had known in the past, particularly Viggo. At the time I had put it down to being starved for attention, to being sex-starved, to its being a fantasy about someone safe who could perhaps gratify those of my needs that had never been fully met. A housewife doesn't have many male acquaintances, so in a situation where my marriage was far from happy, it was natural for me to reach back into the past and fantasise about an unfinished love. I believed that Viggo had loved me the way I had loved my husband, and I trusted that he would never really forget me. I had always planned to look him up so I could show him how dull and worn out I had become, and give him a chance to cease dreaming of me in case he still held a torch for me.

But then I found out that Viggo really *had* continued loving me. Perhaps this new rush of love that I felt was just pure gratitude that someone still found me attractive, that it might once more transform me into an exciting and mysterious being. Perhaps my feelings were stirred up, relieved that someone could feel so strongly, that such emotions could be directed at me again, an unfamiliar man loving an unexplored, new me. The excitement of the unknown in itself was a pleasure, as we were virgins to each other. There might have been many other reasons why the spark had been lit between us. Perhaps the flame had never really died out; perhaps it was because we were both sad and lost at that particular time; perhaps it was because a relationship between us had fewer barriers because of our shared history and past feelings for each other.

One thing, however, was how we felt about each other. Quite another was the thought of changing partners. That frightened us both. It was true that the unquestioning love for our spouses was no longer there, only the tired feeling of knowing one's partner's shortcomings. Then there was the insecurity of not knowing whether our own faults might be unacceptable to someone else, the fear of not being able to live with a new partner's faults, and that maybe our feelings weren't strong enough to weather these. Too much was at stake. But no matter which angle I viewed it from, which explanation was the best fit, which excuse could be most reasonably accepted, I loved him. And yes, he loved me too. Maybe not as crazily as the last time he had seen me, maybe also more cautiously because his feelings had not been returned at the time. But I knew that now it was not a dream of me he loved.

No, he loved the adult me, the real me, flaws and all.

*

That night I thought about how we had made love. I didn't feel dirty or cheap, instead I thought about how amazing it had been. That was the worst of it. I had expected nothing, or that it would be good. But I had not expected the depth of feeling, the ecstasy we had reached simultaneously. Despite this, we had agreed not to meet again, but I thought it was crazy to just leave it at that. I thought that we should explore our feelings now, live with them for a while, and reach some decision. To end it here was premature.

Very romantic, very clean, to experience each other once or twice and never again. But that could only succeed with a chance acquaintance. This was us. We were too involved, we knew each other too well, and we had known and thought about each other for almost half our lives. It seemed almost poetic justice for us to have had each other at last. I thought maybe we could marry when my children grew up, maybe when my husband and Viggo's wife died. But no! We were young *now*, our blood was boiling *now*, and it *had* to be now!

How decent he was, sickeningly decent! What kind of a hold did his wife have over him, anyway. Why did she insist on keeping his body—because surely, she knew that his soul was mine? He said that he had asked her for a divorce, told her that I was back and that he loved me. He said that he loved her too, but not in the same way. She had thrown things, and shouted, and in the end, she had broken down and cried, saying that she loved him. It apparently didn't matter to her that he didn't return her feelings to the same degree. She had pointed out how well matched they were in so many ways. And then he had thought about my little family and how they needed me, and how she needed him, that he was all she had, and he decided never to see me again. How heroic, how steeped in good old Danish common sense—but how unrealistic. What about me and him and our raging feelings and *our* relationship? Didn't that deserve to be considered? What of those few, lighthearted, happy, fleeting times spent together? What about joy?

I thought of his sudden explosive laughter, which seemed to almost hurt him, breaking the melancholy face into a thousand happy wrinkles, his big white beautiful teeth, and his strong and straight shoulders. I thought of my reflection in the mirror, my millions of tears forgotten and replaced by a clean, young, beautiful expectation settling on the weary worry lines of my face. I thought of the last few mornings which had been surprisingly filled with hope and expectation, free from the habitual exhausted anguish of another day to be faced. There were a million tiny forces in me that warned me not to end it now, to let it work itself out to its conclusion instead of leaving it at this breathless stage with an eternal question mark of what could have been.

Didn't his wife realise that it was impossible, unthinkable, to end it here? The end would surely have to be determined by him or me, by us alone. I knew he could not forget me now. How could she live with the faraway expression on his face that meant so much more than his mere physical presence? Well, I wouldn't call him; it would only make matters worse. It was his decision, so he would have to change that decision, not me.

It was night. I was lying in bed, unable to sleep, looking at how the street light from the window reflected on the ceiling. I watched the strange moving patterns that the headlights of a car threw up there, the approach and finally the disappearance of it. And I thought of his hands, his face, his thighs, and his burning kisses. The lighthearted playful way we had made love. It wasn't at all what I had imagined an affair to be like—intense and heavily sexual. He had been leaning on his hands high above me, his arms on either side of me, locking me in beneath him.

'Well, you got me at last, didn't you,' I said with a naughty look in my eyes.

'Yes, now I'm up here. What are you going to do about it?' he replied, his shiny white teeth flashing in a devilish grin.

In response, I had stretched my arms above my head, relaxing completely beneath him. I closed my eyes. He chuckled. I looked up again and saw his gorgeous broad, almost hairless, chest above me, covered with perspiration. Sweat drops were gathering on his chin. I could trace them from the wet lines leading from his forehead and cheeks. His eyes were joyful, triumphant, he was really enjoying this. And I was glad it was like this, the first time. There was no pretence. Neither of us was trying to show off about how sleek we might be at lovemaking. It had been a slow, soft, joyful, tender, and sensual exploration.

The ceiling above me flickered and moved and brought me back to the present once more. I closed my eyes and recalled the woods, so soft in their fine greenery, the twigs crunching under our feet as we searched for a private spot, our hands locked together, protecting each other from the feelings of the parting that would follow. The hum of a million insects in the soft, soft grass, the sun dappling the leaves, the shadows of a leaf upon another, one dark, the other light green. The terrible beauty of the lightest of green …

*

Days passed. It was 8 o'clock. He was still at home, he could call me, he wouldn't be able to stop himself, the phone was there, and I would be answering it. Time passed. Now he would be at the office, and later again, it was almost time for him to be back at home. I would call him. No, he must call me. What if he was really happy that it was so easily over, and he could let it run off him like water off a duck's back? What if I called him and he was rude? I would call. So what if I did? The trapped feelings propelled my impulsiveness. Apparently, I needed a slap in the face before I would give up. I knew I would get hurt. What would he think of me? What kind of a woman was I, running after him when I should be busy with my little children, engaging with my husband? I couldn't call from my father's phone. My husband would hear me even though he might not understand Danish. Lili, my stepmother, would be angry with me for carrying on like this, she would not allow it. The children were noisy, running around.

I told my family I was going downstairs to buy some Danish pastries. There was a phone booth just around the corner. I dialled his number, and then his voice was saying, 'Hello?' Again, this silly feeling that I didn't really need him, so what was I calling him for?

'Hi, it's me. I'm sorry I called, but I miss you.'
'It's all right. I miss you too.'
'Have you been thinking about me?'
'Yes.'

'Look, I've thought about this. It's crazy. Let's see each other again. It's the only way to find out how we really feel.'

'Maybe. Although I've been feeling rather good about it being over, but maybe you are right. Can I see you Friday?'

'No, not Friday, I have to go shopping for clothes for the children.'

'When then ... tomorrow?'

'No, I can't. I can't think of an excuse to get away. How about the weekend?'

'No, I can't then, Gilla is home and we always do everything together.'

'Can't you drop her with a friend and say you want to go for a drive by yourself?'

'No, I never do things like that. It would be too obvious, and anyway, she doesn't really have any friends.'

'Oh, all right, forget it. It's no good like this anyway, sneaking around. I guess the best thing is if we don't see each other anymore after all.'

'Yes, I guess it is.'

'Goodbye, then. But don't forget, I think I love you. I know it sounds crazy, but I think I do,' I said.

'Goodbye, Mimi.'

When I got back upstairs to my father's apartment, everyone had a strange expression on their faces. My husband asked me where I had been. I said at the baker's.

'Why did you have to go downstairs to make a call? Is there anything you want to conceal from me? We never used to do that before!'

'How did you know?'

'The kids wanted to follow you and when they couldn't find you, I went downstairs to help them. I saw you in the phone booth.'

Sprung, yet I didn't even care.

'Oh, well, if you really want to know, I just called Viggo and told him that we had better not meet again.'

'Why couldn't you do it from up here?'

I looked at my husband briefly before replying. It was an honest reply. 'Because I didn't think Lili would approve,' I said, and turned my face away from his gaze.

CHAPTER 6

A few days later, Michael and I were invited to visit a couple of old friends. While my husband was busy at the playground with the children, I confided in my girlfriend. As I described the situation, I saw it all clearly. My friend thought that there was no use staying in a marriage until the parties ended up hating each other. I knew somehow that we were on the verge of that. There *was* no way back for us. I decided to call Viggo as soon as I got back to my father's place.

Once again, I called him from the phone booth. It was a Saturday and his wife would be at home. They were planning to go away the next day for a two-week holiday. Two weeks seemed like an eternity. I had to tell him now. His wife picked up the phone. I had not prepared myself for that, or thought of what I would say. I asked to speak to her husband.

'Who is this?'

'It's Mimi.'

'Why are you calling? Don't you think it would be better to leave the past be?'

'Well, he called me too. I just want to speak with him for a moment.'

'But what for? Don't you think …'

And then his voice interrupted, shouting, 'Put that damned phone down, Gilla!'

'Okay, well you heard him. I have to put the phone down.'

I beat her to it and staggered out of the phone booth, the wine from lunch somewhat numbing my pain. I walked back, feeling as if my body was a void and air could pass right through me. A million thoughts were circling around my head. How could he, oh, how could he? Surely, I hadn't been that disgusting. Surely, I wasn't such an awful person. If he had only known why I had called, what I had decided … And now … it would never be …

And yet, I waited every day. I worked out when he would have returned from his holiday. There was no phone call, no letter, no sign. My indignation grew, my pride bled. I felt cheap and used. How could he finish it this way? It hurt deeply.

My reflection in the mirror frightened me. I constantly looked as if I had been crying. The worry lines reappeared. I had no appetite and lost weight. The fatigue returned; my head was no longer held proud and high. Grey endless days crept by. And yet, there was a slow but growing flutter of expectation ... if he rang me, I would tell him. I would tell him to leave me alone! I might even get my husband to do it!

But it wasn't necessary. He didn't call. He didn't write, he didn't care. He didn't even call so I could tell him to leave me alone! Every time I went for an errand downstairs, I scanned the streets for his car and my heart beat faster when I spotted one similar to his.

One day during this time, Michael and I decided to take the children to the woods. The air was cool, the sun was shining palely and tentatively. As we walked, a clearing appeared ahead, a vastness of soft grass, nature's carpet. I took my shoes off and allowed each blade of grass to caress my feet in a soft green greeting. It felt heavenly, but I hated that my steps had to squash their softness. Suddenly, I had the urge to take off all my clothes and become one with it all. I threw my pants and top aside and after a few seconds, I shed my bra—we were in Denmark, after all—not caring who might walk past and look, what anyone might think. Anyone, that is, except my husband. I felt shy and embarrassed in front of him as he watched on with a perturbed expression on his face. It felt almost like some kind of a war dance, some type of shedding of more than my bra, shedding chains perhaps. I didn't know quite what, but I feared that my husband could see more than I myself knew or understood.

I wished *he* were there instead, that we were there alone together. I decided that Viggo and I had to make love once, like this. It would be magnificent to open my eyes and look into his brown ones, then at the brown of the bark, at the green leaves filtering the vast blue above, to feel almost forced down on the ground by this vast blue gravity, to feel part of nature, doing what was natural. I started to roll around in the grass, heady, high, and giddy. The children saw me and their delighted squeals announced their approach. I saw their faces above me, and I loved them. They were my offspring, they were part of me, they looked like me, they were laughing. I had never felt as close to feeling like their mother as I did then. They lay draped all over my near-naked body and we rolled together, rolled and rolled until I felt dizzy, the trees silently dancing on the horizon, the sky bearing down. The pressure of the sky made me feel pure abandon. I lay heavily against the ground, spread-eagled and out of breath, laughing helplessly, panting from the effort. The children were dancing around me, their little heads touching the sky, begging for more.

But I couldn't, I was spent. This was my love-dance, but where would it lead me? Just then I didn't care, it didn't even matter if 'we' never happened. Yet, the thought of endless days ahead without him sent my mind into unending greyness. I wouldn't have just rolled around here if it had not been for him. I wouldn't even have noticed that the sun was still shining ...

*

Then we all went away for a two-week holiday to Hungary so we could visit family in Győr, where I was born. It was the first time I had been back since 1956 when I'd fled from the Hungarian Revolution as a small child. For me, Hungary was a very dark place, a place of indescribable abandonment, loneliness, longing, and terror. All during our stay, I felt like a cat on a hot tin roof, ready to flee in case there was the slightest sense of danger, even though the revolution was long over. Every day, I wondered anxiously whether we would be prevented from leaving at the end of our time there, and I only relaxed once we were on the plane back to Copenhagen.

The evidence of communism was everywhere. There were the brutal grey buildings, but also the officials who used their positions in abusive ways.

Soon after arriving, I went to see a doctor when my baby, who had probably picked up on my anxiety, developed acute bronchitis for the first time in her life. The doctor immediately yelled at me, asking why I hadn't brought the child in sooner. She accused me of having known about the illness for a long time (which was, of course, completely untrue). I was taken aback by her rudeness, her confidence in speaking to me like that, and her total absence of boundaries. I reflected on the poor Hungarians who had stayed after the revolution and were subjected to such treatment. But I also met with real kindness, such as an older woman with a scarf who saw my confusion and distress as I walked out of the surgery, and who sought to console me and accompanied me to the local pharmacy. Perhaps the rough and unfair treatment by officials had in turn engendered kindness and solidarity amongst members of the community.

I didn't think about *him* much during that time, too busy exploring my hometown, which was also where my father was born, and meeting family and other important people from my parents' past. It was exciting to get to know my close family members as an adult and to see my cousins and our children mingle and play. They were the only family I had, as the majority had been gassed during the Second World War, and being with them was heart-warming and restorative. But even while on the trip, I occasionally pictured the mail slot in the front door of our apartment in Copenhagen and wondered if there might be a letter for me.

When we returned, I ran up the stairs with a mixture of fear and anticipation, hoping yet trying to prevent any disappointment by telling myself that of course he wouldn't have tried to contact me. Wasn't it quite obvious from that dreadful evening in the phone booth? But no, I could not believe that. He had loved me for 11 years, desperately. That kind of love could not just die. There had to be an explanation. He couldn't be that weak, to let his wife end this affair. Marriage or no marriage, she had no right to butt in, he was an individual person, after all. I was certain that he hadn't asked her to pick up the phone in case it was me calling. They had probably been busy packing for their holiday, and had made up. Anyway, he had told me it was over ... and then I had called him. He was probably angry with me, hadn't wanted to spoil what they were trying to patch up ...

I felt worthless, even whorish. Once inside, I was empty, and later I let my husband make love to me. It was all right, it didn't matter; nothing did. I could manage without *him*. I could even be unfaithful to his love—with my husband. The days passed. I thought of calling his mother and decided against it. She would know no more than I. He wouldn't have confided in her. Since he had been hospitalised, and the psychiatrist had indicated that his mother was partly to blame for his condition and that he should stay away from her, they saw each other too rarely for that. Yet as the days passed, somehow my expectation grew.

*

My father suffered a heart attack and had to be hospitalised. It turned out not to be very serious. As the hospital was close by, I went to see him at least once a day. The streets became secretive places. Had he been driving past recently? I scanned the parked cars, and the cars on the road. I felt watched all the time. I thought of nothing but him. We were due to return to Australia shortly, maybe in a week. The walks to the hospital were a pleasure, the trip back exciting, full of promise that I might see him on the way. I felt he had to make a move. I mulled over in my mind the events, the words we had spoken, a thousand times, first examining them coldly, then lovingly, longingly. The solutions I came to as I neared my father's place were never the same. At times I decided that he had meant to be so rude as to hurt me, to make me realise that it was over. At other times I knew he was suffering and longing for me. Each day my heart beat a little faster.

Then Michael broached the idea of taking our eldest daughter on a trip on their own during our last remaining week in Denmark. I agreed. We made plans for his trip. The Saturday before they were to leave, I returned from visiting my father at the hospital to find that there was a message for me from Viggo. He had called and would call again shortly. It almost didn't surprise me. But it was useless to try to hide my feelings. It had been more than two whole months. So I was right: he *had* been yearning all this time. My cheeks felt suddenly flushed, I could tell my eyes lit up, I couldn't even contain the bubbling giggle in my throat and let it out in an unchecked roar of laughter. I would have my revenge. It had been a long time since I'd told a man where to go …

I went into the kitchen where I could be alone a moment, to control my emotions, to sort out what this meant, and to think about what to say to him. Perhaps I would say, 'Look, why don't you concentrate on your wife,' and then slam down the receiver, or 'What do you want from me? Leave me alone.' I considered calling out to my husband to take the call and tell him to say one of those things. But immediately, I had an image of the situation, a split second of imagined panic, slamming down the phone but then changing my mind—how could I call him back then? Finally, I decided I would just ask him what had happened when I'd called the last time, and who did he think I was! I decided I would hear him out. But even then, I knew I was fooling myself, I had forgiven him a long time before, or maybe I hadn't even been really angry at all. I ran a bath in case he could see me that day. I would demand that he meet up with me. I didn't even bother thinking up an excuse to tell my husband. I would make one up along the way. It wouldn't be believed, anyway.

I bathed, my ears straining to hear the phone. It was already 30 minutes past the time he'd said he would call back. Maybe he had changed his mind, maybe he was relieved I hadn't been home. There was a knock at the bathroom door. My husband was calling from outside to say there was a call for me. I flew out of the bath, half dried myself, and battled with the jumper, dragging it over my damp body while it refused to fit over my head. I left the socks. And yet, I was glad of the delay. Maybe I had wanted it that way. I hadn't run to answer the phone. He would have been embarrassed that my husband had answered the call. I got my cigarettes, an ashtray, a box of matches. My little girl wanted something, my older child was talking with him on the phone. The children loved talking on the phone. I let the time drag. My voice to my little girl was calm, reassuring, dawdling almost. He would be hearing me in the background. Finally, I forced the receiver out of the older child's reluctant hand.

'Hello?' I drawled, sounding very cold, bored. 'Don't you owe me an apology? What do you want, why are you calling?'

His tortured voice, excusing, wretched, almost childishly whining, said, 'An apology? Maybe I do. I don't even know what I wanted to talk with you about. I just wanted to hear your voice.'

'Well, now you have heard it.'

I was cruel and defiant. I had the upper hand.

'How did you know we were still here?'

'I have my means.'

'How?'

'I passed your apartment a couple of times and saw that your curtains were still hanging in the windows. New tenants would have hung their own curtains, so I thought you would still be here. You've been away, too.'

'Well, I must say! Have you tried to call before?'

'Yes, but you were never home.'

Then abruptly I asked, 'Why did you let your wife slam the phone down on me?'

'It wasn't like that. Do you really believe that?' His voice picked up, almost cheerful at my mistaken belief.

'Oh, come on. I heard you shout at her to put the phone down. Do you think I deserve that? Am I the kind of woman you can do that with?'

'Look, it wasn't like that. Hear me out. She wouldn't stop talking to you and I couldn't talk to you until she put down the receiver. I didn't want her to listen in.'

'How could you speak with me if she put the phone down?'

'On the other receiver, of course.'

'Oh, likely story.'

'It's true. I was downstairs at the phone and she picked it up upstairs. When she put the phone down, she disconnected the call. We had a hell of a fight afterwards. I tried to phone you the day after.'

'No, she didn't. I put the phone down first.'

Now I believed him.

'Well, I couldn't get onto you, and then we went away.'

'How was the holiday?'

'Very pleasant. We ended up somewhere in Poland.'

'Oh.'

'I thought it was better if we didn't see each other again, so I decided not to get in touch with you when we got back. I don't know why I'm calling now.'

I had to hurt him once more. 'We're leaving …'

'Yes, I knew you were, sometime. When?'

'In one week.'

There was silence. Then he said with a sigh, 'It's probably for the best, for all of us.'

My voice cracked. 'All of us? I've been missing you so badly. My husband is going away this whole next week. We could have a whole week. See me today, tonight at 8.'

'No, I can't, how about Monday?'

'Oh, I don't know. I probably can't … or won't. I want to see you tonight.'

'It's impossible. Monday?'

'Saturday? Sunday? I can arrange a whole day!'

'I can't.'

'Oh, come on, don't be so damned good all the time! Think of some stupid excuse. You'll find one. We have to meet just one more time before I leave!'

'Monday?'

'Oh, forget it then. We can't start that again. It's better if we don't see each other at all.'

'Yes, I guess so.'

I felt flat, grey, deflated, and yet much, much better. Now I knew how he felt. Now I knew what had happened the night I'd called him to say I wanted to stay in Denmark with him and my little girl. Fate just had to be real. It had been that close!

*

But it didn't end there. Another call followed, and we arranged a rendezvous for the day my husband and eldest daughter were to leave. I spotted him from the window. He came to pick me up too early before my husband left. I mumbled to my husband that I would go down for a bike ride. It was absurd—going for a ride an hour before they were to leave! I rode down the street and around an intersection before riding up to his car. It was the first time I'd seen him in two months. He rolled down his car window, and I asked him to come back for me in an hour.

'I don't have much time. I have to be home by 11,' he said. 'I'm sorry, it can't be helped.'

'Okay, shall we go to your apartment?'

I looked down into the darkness of the car, and caught sight of his eyes. They were shy, forcing their gaze into mine.

'Okay.'

Finally, my husband and daughter left. I felt very uneasy. What if something went wrong, what if they rang home and found that I wasn't there, what if they forgot something in the apartment and came back for it?

I was sitting in Viggo's Mini Moke, speeding over to my family's holiday apartment, while my youngest child was asleep at my father's place, minded by Lili. We sneaked upstairs like naughty children, and then the key in the lock made a metallic echoing rattle in the stairwell, making us freeze. We escaped inside. He grabbed me around the waist and kissed me. And kissed me again.

'I thought you said that once would be enough for a lifetime?' I teased.

'Yes, that's what I thought. I was wrong.'

We both felt bad. This was the bed that my husband and I shared, with *him* in it. What was I doing? Their departure was too fresh to ignore. I couldn't let myself go. Then I heard a car door slam on the street below and stiffened. I disentangled myself from him and rushed to the window. There was no one down there. I ran back to the bed, my heart pounding, keyed up, anxious.

'I'm sorry, I'm really nervous, what if they come back?'

'Don't be sorry, I understand.'

We lay on our backs, side by side. His passion had subsided, and I guess mine hadn't really been there from the start.

'This is completely crazy, it's wrong. What am I doing here with you!'

'Would you rather that we didn't see each other again?'

'Yes, I guess so. It can't lead to anything, anyway, and I just feel cheap like this, it's neither nice nor good. I know I'm going back to Australia and you don't want to leave your wife, so it's no use.'

It seemed so easy to see it that way when I was with him. We got dressed. The atmosphere between us was strained. He drove me back to my father's place.

'Okay. Goodbye, then. Look after yourself and your kids.'

'No, don't say goodbye, we've said that too often, it's almost like a joke.'

'All right then, see you. Is that better? Does it make it easier?'

'Yes.'

I smiled, got out of the car, and didn't look back. I walked up the stairs and felt free, more than ever before. It was *my* decision and it was right. It had to be this way. I regretted nothing. There was nothing to regret.

CHAPTER 7

The days at the palliative care unit are long and exhausting, although all I am doing is sitting next to Viggo's bed. He is sleeping on and off, so I work on Sudoku puzzles to while away the time. We used to play a game of 500 during Viggo's many other hospital stays, but here at the palliative care unit neither of us is motivated to play. I wonder how long the dying process will take, and what to advise the children, as they keep asking the very same question.

School is out, and they want to know if they can go away for a brief holiday with their families or whether they should stay around, just in case. Perhaps the dream Viggo had on the second day he was in hospital holds the clue.

He had been sitting up in bed as he told us about the dream, thinking it was significant, and asked us what we thought it might mean. In the dream he was in Denmark, down in his old bicycle shed, where he had often played as a child. All the bicycles had been removed and replaced by a casket. When he looked closer, he saw that it was his body lying in the casket. Then the dream gave some sort of an instruction, something about the time of death depending on when the doctors removed all the metal supports. We all discussed what the metal supports represented, and when we were out of earshot, we thought we could solve the date if we were able to identify their meaning. Metal rods are used in construction to hold material together and maintain permanence, so the dream probably referred to the life support provided to him by the doctors. How typical for Viggo to dream about architecture as a symbol of his body!

My phone rings frequently with enquiries from friends wanting updates and the best times to come for a visit. The children are also on the phone a lot when they are not with us, asking what they can bring. Rebecca often makes soups for Viggo. But right now I am alone with the Sudoku, and as I can't immediately solve it, my mind returns to our torrid affair.

*

The day after we had decided not to meet again, I woke up and thought, 'Oh no, not another lousy day.' I was in a bad mood, having to organise our return tickets for the following week. But at least having to speak with the travel agent and rush around and start to pack helped fill my emptiness. In the middle of all the activity, I suddenly became aware of being in the apartment where *he* had been the night before. I looked over to the corner where he had dropped his shoulder bag. I shook the sheets for any long, straight, dark hairs. I noticed a spot on the sheet and washed it. I ran a bath, bathed my daughter and then myself. I wanted to soak, to free myself of guilt. But the bath did not help. I didn't really care what I wore. I didn't even want to see my face in the mirror. Then I called my friends to tell them we were leaving and invited them over for a last get-together.

I took my little girl over to my father's place and put her down for her nap. Then I looked at my watch. Four o'clock. He would be home soon. How could he stand not calling me, how could he stand me saying goodbye? I thought of calling him, and then thought the better of it. Lili arrived home from work. She took one look at my face and put two and two together. She wanted to call him and talk to him. I said that was out of the question. If anyone should call, he should. She said that I was a fool and that he was, too. We could have had the whole week. He could have made excuses; everything could have been arranged, somehow. This might be the last time we ever saw each other, we would regret playing at being heroes now. Then suddenly the phone rang. My pale face flushed. I rushed to the phone, frightened that it might go dead in my ear. It was him. Lili smiled and picked up the second receiver to listen.

'Hi, how do you feel?'

'All right, and you?'

'Lousy. I haven't slept all night. I've thought a lot about the whole thing; about us. It's probably better to finish it, to try and save our marriages.'

'Do you miss me?'

'Yes, very much.'

'Then come over.'

'No, I can't, I've got to pick up my wife in a couple of hours.'

'Oh, come on, don't be so terribly Danish! Lili wants to speak with you. Come over!'

A relieved laugh. Then, 'Okay, I'll be there in 15 minutes.'

Lili and I looked at each other. I ran to embrace her, swinging her around.

'You silly kid, you haven't changed these last eight years. But it's good to see you like this. You look just like you did then; you've lost years from your face. You look alive again!'

My friends were due to arrive anytime for my goodbye dinner, and I was hoping he would arrive a little before they did. He did arrive before the guests. I was done with pretending and openly held his hand. He looked shy as he greeted Lili.

Lili said, 'Oh, so we meet again. You have changed, you look very different. You've lost weight.'

'Have I? Maybe I have, that's what everyone says.'

By then, it was time for Lili to go to the hospital to see my father and I asked her to let him know that I would visit in the morning. Then Viggo and I were alone and I covered his face with kisses until he gave in and kissed me back. It was just like it should be. I felt whole again in his company. I drank in the sight of him, his brown eyes, his Beatle cut, his lips; my eyes didn't leave his face. I wondered how he could look anywhere but at me.

One of my old girlfriends arrived and we went into the kitchen. I offered my friend a beer and we drank it straight from the bottle, in the Danish way. He stood there, a bit shy. But now I was in a great mood, giggling. My friend realised what was going on and looked from me to him and back again. Feigning disapproval, she addressed him. 'She hasn't changed, has she?'

'No,' he smiled. There was no reproach, just good-natured teasing. I felt really protected by these people from my past. It was where I belonged, amongst those who cared about me and knew me. My husband did not belong here in this place, with this me ...

Lili returned from the hospital, bringing some of my friends up with her from downstairs. They gathered in the lounge room and I spoke with everyone. I was on a high, my voice was high-pitched, and all the while my attention was in the kitchen where I could see that Viggo and Lili were having a chat. They were out there for a long time. I wondered what they could be talking about. I kept glancing towards the kitchen, all the while gesticulating, conversing with the visitors and making merry. I saw him look down, nod his head from time to time while Lili spoke, then suddenly he embraced her, and they came into the lounge room.

'I've got to go, goodbye everyone,' he said.

'I'll see you down.'

Everyone became strangely quiet. Everyone knew. We walked downstairs together.

'What did Lili say?'

'Probably what she's been saying to you. She is a very clever woman, a wonderful woman, you must talk with her. I'm coming to see you tomorrow. Is that all right? I don't know when I can get away, so I'll call you in the morning. Okay?'

We stood there and kissed.

'Let me go now, I'll be late, we don't want to spoil everything. See you,' he said, and disappeared out the door. I stood there for a minute. Relieved, secure, protected, supported, excited. Slowly, I walked back upstairs. I didn't even care to hide the way I felt, I didn't bother to pretend. My little daughter had woken up and greeted me happily at the door. I didn't feel guilty, I just picked her up and kissed her tenderly. It was all right. Lili approved of it. She had accepted me for the adult I was. Nothing really mattered, only love and happiness. And my happiness could only come from *him* now. During dinner, I laughed a lot, talked incessantly, could feel my eyes shining, my whole body radiating. I saw all these people around me, and I thought that they were only filling in time, that their eyes were grey in comparison. It seemed to me that they looked almost envious of how I had demonstrated my daring affair so freely, of how I did not hide my feelings. And all the while, behind the laughter and chatter, there was a refrain inside me singing over and over, 'He is coming tomorrow, I will see him tomorrow ...'

*

The next day, my little girl and I were supposed to have dinner with a friend so I arranged for Viggo to come sometime during the day. However, he called later that morning to say in a hushed voice that he didn't know when he could get away, but it would be after dinner.

'I've got to go now,' he said.

'Are you calling from home?'

'Yes,' came his strained, hushed voice.

'Hurry. I miss you. I love you.'

'Goodbye.'

I walked over to the mirror, brushing my hair, observing my face. The worry lines that had marked my face so prematurely were almost invisible, and a silly, secretive smile was dancing across my lips. My eyes were crystal clear and shining even under half-closed lids. My cheeks were strangely, becomingly, flushed. I looked like a new woman. My hand was shaking as I brushed my wiry hair and remembered the way he could penetrate me, send me into instant ecstasy. This rush of emotion, just from the sound of the phone, a few seconds of his voice, and his promise to see me today. I wondered how I could hold my head up high, how I could love the way I looked, love the way I felt. But I didn't feel shameful or guilty. Even having my little daughter next to me, watching me brush my hair, only called forth emotions of a fierce female pride in her, *my* flesh, *my* blood.

I told my friend during dinner that I had to leave early to meet Viggo. The steak was almost rare, and I hate rare steaks, but I gulped it down. My friend had two children and I felt so strange in this homely place with nappies here, toys there, my friend's tired face, her husband humouring whingy, tired children, my own aloofness, and my little girl's insecure vibes. I felt that I was cheating my way out of a difficult situation, moving away from the traditional family. I was taking the easy way out, escaping.

Then my little girl and I rushed to the train. When we got off at our station, it was pouring. I had to take a taxi the short distance to my father's place so we wouldn't get wet and so I wouldn't miss Viggo, in case he was on his way. A dozen people were crammed into the doorway to the station behind me, trying to stay out of the rain, all waiting for a taxi. Finally one came, dropping off a passenger. I rushed over and got in. Back home at my father's place, I went out onto the balcony to scan the street below. He wasn't there. I had felt all evening that he wouldn't be coming, and any time spent without him seemed like a complete waste of life. My little one was playing and I went into the kitchen and looked at the few dishes I hadn't washed up after lunch. I could hardly bear the thought of being stuck in the kitchen washing up, feeling compelled to stand on the balcony and wait for him. Then I thought, who cares, it doesn't matter. He is just a chicken, a weakling, he is spineless, and I don't even like him. I can't be that desperate for sex, after all. Defensive thoughts, first learnt as a child to help me through painful disappointments, like the many times my father had failed to keep his promise to pick me up and take me to his place, leaving me with my cold mother and the humiliation of my triumphant stepfather's judgement of my father's many flaws.

I washed up. Slowly. The minutes passed. I walked through the lounge room and over to the balcony, looking casually down one side of the street, then turning my head and scanning the other side. My eyes stopped halfway at the sight of a moving figure in the dark on the other side of the street. I looked more attentively now. A shoulder bag, a shirt open at the neck, windblown dark hair, a hand waving. I froze. And then this gurgling, boiling feeling from somewhere in the middle of my body started rising, rising, and exploding in my mouth in a giggle I could barely hold back. I turned, rushed over to the door, ran down, three steps at a time, and was downstairs before he had quite reached for the buzzer or the door handle.

'I thought you wouldn't come.'

'I wouldn't do that. Do you think that's what I'm like?'

'Oh, it wouldn't have mattered, anyway. I didn't really feel like seeing you today.'

'Oh.'

'Well, what's the use? You don't love me anyway. I don't know why you bother.'

I was hurt that he had made me wait all day, and wanted to hurt him back.

'Look, I'm not in love with you the crazy way I was before. But don't think that you are indifferent to me; can't you see that I'm really suffering? I feel awful, being here, yet I feel awful not being with you. At home I no longer feel I belong, I just yearn to see you. And when I'm with you, I know I should be at home. But let's not stand down here. Let's go upstairs, it's freezing.'

What was he saying? Why didn't he love me like before? Now he seemed unattainable, which made him even more desirable, and I felt exposed, no longer in control of the situation. But more importantly, I hadn't counted on feeling how I had felt when I saw him. I had really believed that it was all some melodramatic play or a holiday fling, that I didn't really feel *that* deeply.

But now I knew. I loved him. I couldn't help looking at him, I had to touch him. The acknowledgement of it sent shivers through me. I was trapped; I was going to get hurt now. The game was over. At first it had just been a devilish little game. But now, tonight, it had become real.

CHAPTER 8

The next day, Viggo had planned to tell his wife that he was going to visit his mother and then come and see me, and I had loosely arranged to visit another friend with my little girl. So I wrote a hasty note with the address and phone number of my friend and secured the note to the back door in case he came early. At my friend's place, I was only physically present, my ears straining for the sound of his steps on the stairs outside. Despite everyone in the room, all the action, the food, and my own outwardly normal interactions, all I could think of was him. When the time came to leave and he had not arrived, my heart became suddenly heavy. I had been in an expectant, hopeful mood throughout the day while at the same time cautioning myself not to expect him just yet. Now I felt deflated, almost depressed.

Once back at my father's place, I walked from window to window, to the balcony, sat down, tried to read, looked at the clock on the wall, and then looked at my watch to double-check the time. He wouldn't come now until after dinner. Disappointed, I thought, *It's too late now*. Danes always eat dinner at 6, I recalled. I hopped up on the bench in the kitchen, finally deciding to sing and play the guitar while my little girl was having her nap. And just then, the buzzer rang. I jumped, hardly knowing how to put down the guitar, how to get to the door fast enough. I pressed the intercom to let him in, paced a few quick steps back and forth in front of the door, then tore it open and started out to meet him halfway. He was just coming up the last flight of stairs when he saw me come out. His jacket was flying out behind him, his dark hair flowed backwards from his forehead, his eyes were velvet, questioning, meeting mine.

He looked shy, as if it was an effort for him to look into my eyes. We entered the apartment together. I wanted to touch him and kiss him, but just then, Lili came out from the bedroom all sleepy. The buzzer had woken her from her nap. She asked whether he could give her a lift to the hospital, as she had overslept and was now running late for my dad's visiting hour. That was no problem, he said. Just then, the little one woke up too and I thought, damn it, he probably has to go home soon, and now she has woken up, and Lili, who could have looked after her, has gone for at least an hour, so we can't even be alone. I made the little one a bath and was just giving her a few toys to play with when he returned. I rushed over and kissed him. He stepped back.

'I'm not in the mood.'
'Why not?'
'I don't know, don't you feel like that sometimes?'
'No, not when I'm with you.'

He sat down in the darkened lounge room and I put *Ninety-nine Ways* on the record player, saying it always reminded me of him.

'Why?'
'I don't know, it just does, and I've been listening to it all day.'

He started to hum along with the tune, as if to try to experience my feelings.

'Did you visit your mother already?'
'Yes, it was one of those French visits.'
'Short?'
'Yes, but it was more than enough time with her.'
'Did you tell her where you were going?'
'Yes. She asked me if I was still in love with you.'
'What was your reply?' The words came out all garbled.
'I said I don't know.'

He had his head in his hands as he sat, his elbows resting on his legs, his hair covering his fingers, so all I could see was the top of his head. I was indignant. My pride was hurt. Here I'd been, hardly able to wait all day and feeling zombie-dead at not having seen him.

'Well, what the hell do you want then? Go away. You love your wife, just go away. You only want this as a casual affair, one that begins and ends. Even the best of marriages has them!'

'Oh, Mimi, don't let's argue in the little time we have together!'

I walked over to him and knelt down, lifting his head, forcing his eyes to look into mine, only an inch away from my face.

'Don't you know how I feel? Don't you feel the same, that all the time away from each other seems endless and a waste of time, a test of patience? Don't you feel that you're only really alive when you're with me, like now?'

I was out of breath, my hands leaving his face and now squeezing his wrists.

'Oh, Mimi, I was so scared of falling in love with you again, I didn't want to, and it's happened anyway. Of course I know what I feel, how I feel, otherwise why should I be so wretched? You have a husband and two little children, and I have a wife. We can't do this, four innocents would be hurt, hurt,

hurt. And do you think we would be happy? Do you think we could last through all that? Can't you see how it would haunt us and turn our love into bitterness?'

The sound of splashing bathwater brought us back to the present. My little girl was probably creating a mini tsunami, pretending that she was swimming in Lili's enormous white tub. The darkened lounge room was filled with the strains of *Ninety-nine Ways*. I stood up and looked down at his head and the dark, almost black hair on the backs of his hands. I wanted to force his head away from his hands, I wanted to make love to him, make him want me in his forceful way, even though I had no right to do so. I stood there helplessly, with the music and his presence pulsing through me. Then, his head lifted until his eyes met mine, his despair and mine intermingling. What could be done when our love was the only tie we had to each other? On the outside, my husband and children were dragging me back to the normality and familiarity of family life, while my insides were tugging at me, urging me, to let the marriage go, my emotions telling me that I belonged with him alone. And his wife was patiently waiting for him to come home from his 'visit to his mother', maybe while doing her chores.

My little daughter appeared in the doorway, wet and naked, bringing with her the scent of Badedas bath salts, a few leftover bath bubbles clinging to her little neck. Fresh from her bath, she transformed our intense gaze from despair to guilt. There she was—the innocent party, the reminder. I wrapped her in a towel and suggested she ask him to dry her. She waddled over to him, legs restrained by the tightness of the towel, and shyly mumbled her request. He didn't understand the baby-like talk, so I translated for him. Then I sat down comfortably in my father's beautiful home and watched him dry her naked little body clumsily, his hands a bit too big and shaky from the privilege my child was bestowing on him, his eyes soft with emotion, a breathless smile on his face. I knew what he was thinking: it could be like this ... The sight of my baby's face—she liked the attention—his hands drying her carefully as if she would break, the expression of concentration on his face ... Then the shrill little voice complaining, breaking the spell, 'My back is wet!'

'You didn't dry her back properly,' I said with a laugh.

'I don't know how, I've never really done this before.'

'Didn't you help your sister once in a while with her children?'

'Yes, but that was long ago, her children are big now.'

'It's just like drying yourself. You wouldn't leave your own back wet, would you?'

I scolded him mildly, unable to completely conceal the wry little smile of superiority that was my right as a mother, taking the towel away from him to finish drying, our heads touching, bent over her, concentrating on this child who might have been ours. The tenderness was overpowering. Slowly, I turned my head and kissed his lips. Our eyes lingered for an eternal second, not wanting to leave each other's face. Just then, Lili let herself in. I went into the kitchen to help her with the evening meal and he carried the plates to the dining table. Then we were sitting there, eating. It seemed so right, the three of us and the child who was occasionally glancing at the TV, at times asking for something. There was the contrast of the feeling of peace while at the same time, my impatience to get away and be alone with him. I could hardly eat fast enough.

'Haven't you finished yet?' I asked, tugging at him until he got up and stood next to me. I kissed my daughter goodnight and told her I was going shopping. I kissed Lili goodbye.

She turned to look at him and said meaningfully, 'Look after her, all right?'

'I will,' he said and took my hand.

Then we were running hand in hand, carefree, down the stairs. We waved to Lili and the little one on the balcony, and then the car sped off away from them. The roar of the motor prevented any conversation between us. I glanced at his profile and placed my hand on his thigh in a gesture that said everything. His eyes were staring straight at the road. He turned his head and his eyes met mine. No words were spoken. We *had* to get to my holiday apartment. The hum of the motor accompanied the melody playing in my head, *There must be ninety-nine ways to do without you, but I can't find one tonight …*

I closed the curtains. He found two candles and lit them. Then we met in the middle of the room in an urgent embrace, as if this was all we were meant to do. We didn't feel guilty anymore, this was all that mattered, this existence, framed by the hours that were ours alone. The candlelight flickered shadows onto his face and I had to look closely to recognise the naked desire in his eyes. I had to lean over to hear the muffled moan escaping his lips. Shaking, I could hardly pull the zipper down on my jeans; his haunted expression as he pulled off his pants; then we were melting together once more, this time with nothing to separate us. Holding hands, we walked over to the bed. I lay down and stretched my arms above my head, letting go of all caution, all binding chains, all defences. I succumbed to the sensation of freedom, floating on the sheets, then became suddenly aware as he penetrated my body with his before the floating began anew. I had to have this, I had to live, now.

Almost unconscious, I heard him whisper gently for me to sit up as he pulled at my arms. My limp body followed somehow. Candlelight flickered across his face when I opened my eyes, climaxing, collapsing against his damp chest. Then through a dream I felt him guide my body, I was lying on my side, his hand pushing at my left leg, positioning me gently, and again we were one. I sobbed, hugging the pillow to my face to muffle the sound. Although I had just come, I could hardly stand the waiting, he had to make me come again, this way. It was beautiful. I was motionless, only my chest was heaving, a heavy ripening feeling and an explosion of pillow, his moan, and the red blackness behind my closed lids. I couldn't breathe or move and I didn't want to, I didn't need to. He stayed inside me, moving gently, and I felt myself simmering. I turned my head back and looked at him. I could feel my hair spread above my head on the pillow, my eyes half-closed, my lips dry.

'I've never ever come so beautifully before, I've never ever felt so fully spent,' I whispered. 'Wasn't it lovely?'

'Ah, yes.'

'You make love beautifully.'

'So do you.'

Slowly, gently, he pulled away and stretched out on his back. We had taken our watches off and I didn't want to know what time it was, I didn't dare to find out. I was willing him to forget, too. We were lying on our backs, touching each other with our fingertips, letting our fingers run up and down along each other's bodies, whispering sweet things. The shadows from the candles danced patterns on the ceiling, the flames visible out of the corners of our eyes. Slowly, I felt the desire warm my body again. It hardly surprised me and I barely noticed that it had crept up on me. My fingers demanded him without my conscious command. Then he was kissing my neck and my breasts, we were moving again, and he was trembling up above me before he went right inside and I came. He stopped, and then started again. I was floating; my body was moving of its own volition; I was hardly conscious.

'Would you like me to come right now?'

'No, don't!'

I panicked upon seeing his devilish face, his teasing, tender smile. I moaned for him not to do it, my head moving wildly from side to side. He was going to explode, and we did, together. We lay motionless for a long time.

'How can I leave this, how? I can't, I just can't,' I whispered.

'This is just sex; it's only one part of life, there is more, much more.'

'But we wouldn't make love, not you and I, if we didn't love each other, you know that.'

'Yes, I know that. But we couldn't make it work. There's something holding me back. You don't know me. You don't know what I'm like when I haven't got a job. I die, and I make everyone around me die.'

'Yes, and I'm very messy. I'm a perfectionist deep inside, but really sloppy on the outside. It doesn't actually matter; there are so many more important things in life. Housework is so secondary.'

'Probably. You should see my place. It is all perfect, and very sterile. I'm sick of it, I want to move.'

'I get into rotten moods. I don't really feel bad inside, I just act as if I do.'

'So do I. I really hurt Gilla's feelings sometimes, I can be very cruel. To protect myself, or maybe to strengthen her, I don't know. But I could never hurt *you*. Trouble is that we both have hearts that are too big—just here,' he said, drawing a circle on his chest with a finger.

Film-like images seemed to appear between us, projected onto his naked chest. My husband's face when I rejected him, the children's curly bouncy heads, the buildings of their future school, the house we had always longed to buy. And then I refocused on his face. Our eyes met, hurt.

'Yes. I've always wanted to adopt a child from a war-torn country. Even before my first baby, we tried, but we were told it wasn't possible at the time. I really want to give six months of my life to a place like that, maybe delivering food or helping with medical care, but I can't now that I'm responsible for my own family. I created my children and I have no right to place myself in danger, or take myself away from them. But I wish we could adopt a needy child and give him or her the same we are giving our own children. I'm a pretty ordinary mother, but I do my best, and I would do that for this child too, provide an ordinary life, a good life. I want to do that, one day.'

'I've been thinking a lot about that, helping people in less developed countries I mean. Although they would probably be better off without our butting in.'

'I don't know. And anyway, could you help butting in?'

'No.'

His fingers were caressing me everywhere. I kissed his eyes, his nose, his lips. There was no desire, only the purest of love. The kind of feeling you can afford when your body is satiated.

'What is the time?'

My throat suddenly ached as I answered that I didn't know. He elbowed himself up and looked at his watch on the table.

'We have to go!'

'Yes.'

A sudden barrier arose between us, a rush of coldness, self-consciousness. I looked at him and saw a stranger in a hurry. I became aware of myself and felt like a messy slut lying in the bed in my little family's holiday apartment. And through the candlelight, the toys scattered on the floor came into focus. They hadn't been there before, somehow.

He went into the bathroom and I jumped out of bed and put on my jumper. I didn't want him to see me naked when he came out. We stared at each other strangely when he emerged. I passed him and went inside to wash. He looked so business-like and efficient, so strong and clean ... and not mine. By the time I returned, he was ready to go. He was even holding his bag.

'Hurry, will you? I promised to be home by 11 at the latest.'

'Of course,' I said, and pulled on my jeans furiously.

'You understand, don't you? If we mess it up now, I won't be able to see you tomorrow.' His eyes were pleading, sorry.

'All right,' I said more gently.

The roar of his car, the heaviness of my heart as we neared my father's place, the reality now in sharp perspective, I wondered whether my baby had fallen asleep okay for Lili. Wondering how flushed my cheeks were, whether I could control the stupid smile on my face in case Lili was waiting up for me. Then a glance at his profile, his eyes staring straight ahead, his strong hand yanking impatiently at the gear stick until the car was at full speed. When we arrived, he stopped the motor. He actually stopped it, I thought, hungering for any gesture or word now, until the next day when we saw each other again.

'Do you think of me at night?'

'Yes.'

'When?'

'Oh, about 11 or 12 when I go to bed. It's private then. No one can see my face or guess at my thoughts.'

'I think about you too, every night. Do you want to think of me tonight at 11:30 exactly? Then I will think of you, and we will know. Goodnight. Say it ...'

'I love you.'

'I love you, too.'

I watched him do a U-turn and leave. He didn't look back. I tried to recollect all that had happened as I walked up the stairs. I let myself in quietly and made my bed on the sofa. Lili had gone to sleep, and so had my little girl. I tried to read a magazine and checked my watch to see if it was time to think of him yet, but I turned out the light a short time later. I would think of him until I fell asleep, I thought, and promptly fell asleep.

CHAPTER 9

Michael and our eldest child returned from their trip one day before we left for Australia, and we decided to use the final day to visit some friends in the country. I wasn't keen to go. The phone might ring, and anyway, I couldn't bear the thought of a whole day in the company of these boring people, these people who weren't *him*. The children were in the middle of a second breakfast—they could eat all day if we let them—when the phone rang. Instinct told me it might be him. My eldest daughter beat me to the phone, but before she could hear who was on the other end, I took the receiver from her, telling her it would be a girlfriend.

It *was* him. He sounded excited. 'I've managed to get away for a whole day.'

'But I can't meet you!' I exclaimed in Danish. 'We're leaving in half an hour. We're going to the country. You should have told me before. How did you manage to get away for the whole day? I thought you said you couldn't get away on weekends?'

'I had a great idea. I said I was going fishing. I haven't done that in a while. Come on, I'll be there in quarter of an hour.'

'All right, I'll meet you downstairs. But don't park outside. Go a bit further down the street.'

I had no idea how I could possibly get away. I was becoming very careless. No one would have flushed cheeks and sparkling eyes from speaking with a girlfriend on the phone. Nor would the conversation have been so brief. But I didn't let that worry me. It was up to others what they thought. All I could do was come up with an excuse that might be acceptable to everyone. My husband had stopped asking questions. It was as if he'd rather not know. It was a strange game we were playing, me lying and he accepting the lies, while we both knew the truth. It was obviously one of the many strange games that married folk might play. It was just sad that most of the games had to be painful ones.

My heart was beating in anticipation of this unexpected opportunity to drink in the sight of *him* again. He had called after all! I did mean enough to him that he had come up with a scheme, a big lie, one that would take up the whole day!

I glanced at my watch nervously and tried to think of ways to get out of today's excursion. But there wasn't any; I couldn't stay away. If only part of the family turned up, it would upset the people we were visiting. The problem was that now, the thought of the day ahead seemed even duller than before. I would be there filling in time, knowing that he would be fishing somewhere, thinking about me. I recalled the tender peace between us when we had slept in each other's arms years before as teenagers, and of moments shared more recently, the glances, the unspoken words.

I thought of the kisses that we could have shared today. I felt proud that I could disappoint him; it would fire his love for me to know that I wasn't always available when he wanted to see me. It was good that way. I didn't trust myself to have the strength or the desire to play such a tactical game, but circumstances had forced me to do so.

I had already promised to visit my father in hospital before we left for the day, and it was now time to go. As I rode my bike towards the hospital, I saw the Mini Moke speeding towards me and then swiftly past. There was a girl with blonde hair flowing in the wind sitting in the passenger's seat next to him. It must be his wife. He had come early and was in a real hurry, and the visit to my father had not even taken place. I paid a very short visit and was not really present, getting up and sitting down again, fidgeting. In the end, my father sensed my impatience and told me to go if I had to. I wrapped my arms around him lovingly and with a guilty glance at his warm expression, the twinkle in his eyes indicating that he was enjoying my naughty escapades, I promised another visit after we returned from the country outing.

Then I was flying down the stairs, the hospital lift far too slow. I jumped on the bike and rode as fast as I could. Tears caused by the wind were stinging my eyes, giving me double vision. I was hurrying to meet him, my body leaning forward on the bike, just to be with him for an extra breathless second, to fly into his arms, to be held by him. I spotted his car parked a short distance away from my father's apartment. He was pacing, looking towards the apartment, his body leaning that way as if in readiness to meet me. Our eyes met and I rode into a side street. He got into his car and followed.

'What took you so long?'

'I couldn't get away. We've got exactly 10 minutes together,' I puffed, feeling silly, wind-blown, like a runaway teenager.

'Oh.' He sounded terribly disappointed, his eyes glued to my face, with that shy sideways look that gave his glance even more intensity, as if his willpower to look at me had succeeded over his shyness.

'Here is my mother's and stepfather's address in case you need to contact me. We're going to stay temporarily with Michael's father until we find a house to rent. Shall we walk?'

I pulled the bike alongside us. He told me to park it. I looked around guiltily, then leant the bike against a hedge and hid against his chest. His strong arms immediately enveloped me. I could smell his soap-smell and gently nuzzled his neck with my lips where it was scarred from his morning shave.

'Shaved for me?' I mumbled, as I looked at the collar of his shirt and wondered whether his wife had ironed it for him before he left that morning. It smelled clean, like washing powder mixed with hot ironing.

He sniffed me in return, 'Ahhh, Mimi-smell,' he teased, smiling.

I kept looking around nervously, then at my watch, sharply aware of the ridiculousness of the situation. He must have guessed my thoughts.

'It's really strange having you next to me, taking an unhurried stroll which has to end in minutes, trying to make it feel reasonable, when it's completely crazy.'

I was fidgety and nervous and wanted to go home. I glanced at him and he was a stranger. I had no claim on him, I had no right to him, and he had no hold over me. I thought again how crazy it was to keep on meeting. When I was away from him, I missed him desperately and my heart fluttered feebly, waiting, waiting. Yet, when I was clandestinely with him, it seemed sordid and wrong.

'We're leaving tomorrow and we have to end it here. I really mean it this time. These meetings haven't led anywhere. It's become ever more obvious on each occasion how wrong it all is, how purposeless, empty, and silly. When we don't talk, we just want to hear each other's voices. Then we just want to see each other, and then *that* isn't enough, either. What we really want is to be together all the time, and that isn't possible. If we had no ties, there would be nothing stopping us, and nothing to lose. But we cannot risk that now, nor can we inflict pain, maybe permanently, on the people involved with us, while we make up our minds. Maybe everybody has a dream like the one we've silently shared over the years, maybe it's just a safety valve. Perhaps it's a way of keeping ourselves intact in marriage, keeping a certain dreamy distance from the practicality of life. Maybe we should just keep it a sweet dream. I will always think of you. I always have, especially in bad times. You were my escape. The dream might be shattered if it became reality, and the people who love us and who we love would be forever scarred. Do I make sense?'

'Yes,' he said, 'I have often thought about that, especially since you arrived. I don't feel towards you the way I did when we were younger. It was a wild thing, desperate and exciting, a dreadful love. My feelings towards you now are much more sensible. You could say that I am not as much in love with you as I was.'

'You probably love your wife, and *I* am the habit, the thought-habit.'

'I don't know. Maybe I don't love her at all. Maybe I'm just used to her.'

I could tell that as he was putting these emotions into words, he wanted simultaneously to shrink away from finding out that his relationship with his wife might be based on a lie. Perhaps he was regretting that he had expressed the thoughts. It would be too painful if they were true and now, they could no longer be ignored.

'My wife and I make a sensible couple. We have a lot of physical things in common.'

'What do you mean, physical things?' I asked, wondering whether he might not have enjoyed our lovemaking as much as I had.

'Well, we have all the earthly things in common. We have the same taste in almost everything. And maybe the problem is that I've completed my degree and there's nothing for me to look forward to anymore. We live such a "good" life, so well planned, so sensible—so dull.'

'Do you call this sensible living?' I looked down teasingly at our clasped hands swinging between us in rhythm to our gait. He smiled that shy smile, looking down. He looked depressed and beaten at his last admissions about the state of his life. The dream was almost broken. Dreams must not be analysed or thought about too much. They were useful for keeping *feelings* alive, exchanging the dreary, rational, day-to-day for hope of a more exciting future. Dreams should be unattainable, always craving fulfilment. But if the dream became reality, it might be an anti-climax, with no dreams left to dream.

I looked into his eyes. It hurt to be the sensible one, and it hurt to hear that what we had was just a dream.

'Maybe you should try to persuade your wife to have children after all. Try to make her understand that you need something you can always look forward to, something ever-changing, your *own* extension, and your flesh and blood. There is nothing that makes a person's life more worth living. Children force you to be present, to live fully, and to love. Of course, parenthood has a lot of disadvantages. Impulsiveness, irresponsibility, perhaps even part of your personality, freedom ... all that goes or is curtailed. But you gain something terribly important: the will to live, a purpose. You no longer have to make up or seek out one distant goal after another. You can't imagine how beautiful it is to wake up in the morning, cranky and tired, and be greeted by a gurgling, laughing baby bouncing in its cot, happy just to see you—as you are, dishevelled from lying in bed, or moody. It's hard not to respond to such an invitation to life, to the importance of yourself to that baby, to your baby's unquestioning adoration and need for you.'

I felt my eyes shining as I spoke. Everything I said was true. I was looking forward to life, to its many crevices, its ups and downs, its problems coming from without, not from within.

'Maybe you're right. But I never felt like having a child with my wife ...'

I placed a finger on his pillow-soft lips. I had to go. We agreed not to contact each other. It was best if we settled back into our marriages. It was the most sensible option.

'Promise me to always love me and think of me!'

'I don't have to promise you that. I did, always, and I will.'

I got on the bike and hurried away. Before I turned the corner, I looked back one last time. He was just standing there, with a whole day to spend on his own, arms by his sides, watching me leave.

Again.

CHAPTER 10

Yes, I had left him more than once, but this time I did not think I would ever see him again. Even though each time we parted, we had always somehow managed to reconnect across time and space, I didn't think it would happen this time. This time, it was different. This time, he was leaving *me* and I would never be able to find him again. I glanced towards the bed and admitted to myself that I could not imagine life without Viggo somewhere on the planet.

The first time I'd left was a few short months after we met, and he couldn't bear to watch me go. So why was I now destined to be the brave one, having to let *him* go? How would I be able to survive without my soulmate and my best friend, my personal adviser, my admirer, my lover, my muse?

No one knew me like he did. I would often playfully ask him why he'd stayed with me during the times when I was cold and rejecting, or when I drank and smoked, or when I let loose and screamed at him or at the children out of frustration. His answer was always the same. Just like Michelangelo with his block of the David marble, he knew it was not the real me. He could see through my armour into my real self, which was obviously hidden, even from me. It was that real me he had recognised when we first met.

The story of our initial meeting became quite famous amongst family and friends, who would request to hear it again and again and ask probing questions in order to squeeze out every last detail. So when Viggo's health forced him to become home-bound, he decided to write it all down, and through a lucky coincidence, an abbreviated version became the opening chapter of a recently published book about the Danish 60's pop culture.

Over the years, we often talked together about how we met. These frequent recollections continually anchored and rekindled our belief in our relationship. We always highlighted the magic moment when our eyes met and locked, as if we had somehow found something we had never lost. The secret to our relationship, the deep feeling of belonging, could be found in those first brief hours spent together amidst overwhelming emotions. We both took unusual personal risks and made ourselves vulnerable in order to get to know each other, and that was how we established mutual trust and a lasting connection.

※

I sense some movement and look up from my reverie to see someone standing in the open doorway. It is Abby, the daughter of long-time friends. We have not seen her for months. How sweet of her to come! I invite her in and she sits down opposite me on the other side of Viggo's bed. Her face remains unchanged at the sight of Viggo. What an amazing young woman she has become! I am impressed by her courage in making the visit by herself and admire the way she covers up the shock she must surely feel at seeing the change in his emaciated frame. Her confident and outgoing bubbliness brings a fresh breath of youthfulness into the morbid, sanitised, and impersonal room.

We all chat for a while. And then she asks, 'How did you meet again? I find it such a fascinating story.' I search around and pass across the bed Viggo's original manuscript, which has just been returned to us after making the rounds amongst the nursing staff. 'Why don't you read it aloud to us?' I suggest to Abby. 'Is that okay, Viggo?' I ask, tucking my hand into his where it lies resting on his bed cover. His hot, thin fingers squeeze mine gently.

Abby, who, like all other visitors, feels powerless in such a situation and wants so much to help or do something for us, happily obliges.

'Are you sure you want to?' I ask.

But she is keen; it's very much her thing. She is a musician who has also dabbled in theatre productions. She flicks through the pages. 'It's not that long,' she says, and begins to read.

*

It all started when we were sitting around at Jørgen's place making plans for the evening. It was Saturday so there was no school. Jørgen suggested we should go to Mælkepoppen. I didn't know much about it and nor did Jan, but Jørgen had been there before and told us that it was a place where they served milkshakes and played the latest pop music at Strøget near Rådhuspladsen (Copenhagen's town square). 'There are a lot of young people there and maybe we can meet some girls,' Jørgen said eagerly.

Jan thought it was a great idea, but I wasn't sure. After all, I had a girlfriend and I wasn't interested in meeting someone else. I felt guilty going out without her, but then again ...

'Come on, Viggo, there's no harm in just listening to the music,' Jørgen added as if he had read my thoughts.

It was the middle of November and getting cold. I wore my suede leather jacket and a black leather vest with matching tie. Leather clothes were cheaper in Sweden, so my mother and I had gone to Helsingborg earlier in the year to shop. 'Big enough to grow into,' she had said, being very practical as usual. To complete the outfit I wore my black shoes that had just been fixed.

I remember how one day, I had gone to the cobbler with my old dancing shoes and asked him if he could add an inch to the heels, because it was the latest fashion and I couldn't afford new ones. His basement workshop was just down the road where Niels Ebbesensvej runs into HC Ørstedsvej. I knew him well and apart from fixing our shoes, he used to repair my schoolbag when the sewing came apart, which it often did, as it was handed down to me from the youngest of my two older sisters, and by the time it came into my possession it was already well worn.

The cobbler was an old man with large strong hands and a humped back that spoke of long hours labouring over the sewing machine and the polishing wheel. At first, he didn't want to have anything to do with it. He looked me squarely in the eye and gave me a long sermon about how it would ruin an otherwise fine pair of shoes. He spoke with authority, from a life dedicated to his trade. You wouldn't want to argue the finer points of shoemaking with this man.

But I did. I told him about The Beatles who had topped the music charts and how they were wearing that type of shoes. He just shook his head, but I must have been quite persuasive, for a couple of days later I was the proud owner of a beautiful pair of shoes with high heels and pointed toes.

We stepped off the bus at Rådhuspladsen and walked across to Strøget, which had been turned into a pedestrian mall earlier that year. By that time, I was getting quite excited, for I wasn't used to going out. It was actually the first time and I didn't quite know what to expect. I felt kind of adult, even though it was only a milk bar.

At 16, we couldn't go to a real bar where they served alcohol. Instead, we used to go to private parties, with our classmates taking advantage of someone's parents going away for the weekend, usually with their permission, but sometimes without. These parties, which were fuelled by alcohol acquired after hours through the back door of the local grocer, deteriorated gradually as the night wore on from too much dancing, drinking, and pent-up sexual energy.

Mælkepoppen was located on the first floor of an old four-storey building. Loud music and excited voices greeted us as we made our way up the stairs. People were pushing, eager to get inside. It was a large space with a lot of young people sitting at small tables drinking milkshakes and talking, as Jørgen had described. Their voices blended with the music, produced by a disc jockey standing behind a counter operating a turntable, with an air of importance as he lowered the stylus over the spinning vinyl records. He seemed to attract considerable attention, especially from the girls, who competed for him to play their favourite pop song.

The walls were decorated with posters showing images of the various milk temptations on offer. Smart looking girls dressed in red and white were serving mountains of ice cream and milkshakes over the counter, which stretched halfway down the side wall opposite a row of windows facing the street.

As I was waiting to get inside, a pair of smiling eyes met mine and held them for what seemed like an eternity. I just stood there, and nothing else existed except those eyes and the beautiful face to which they belonged. My heart raced as if it was going to jump out of my chest, and my leather jacket suddenly felt awfully hot. Had I known then that what was about to unfold would mark a turning point in my life—the beginning of a lifelong journey to discover the true meaning of love—would I have shied away or even understood what that meant?

Shouting above the music, Jørgen brought me back to my senses, 'Come on, Viggo! What are you standing there for? Let's go inside.'

'There's this girl,' I said, choking on my words while trying to control my emotions, 'she's looking at me.'

'Where, where is she?'

'Over there at the table next to the window. She has dark hair and she's wearing a knitted blue jumper. It looks like she's with two other girls,' I said, looking in her direction.

Jan had picked up on the conversation. 'What are you going to do, are you going to talk to her?'

'I'm not going to *do* anything, I can't just walk over there and talk to her.' *Or could I?*

We found an empty table at the far end of the room and I cast a sideways glance at her as we walked past their table. She didn't look up. By the time we had bought our milkshakes and sat down, I had lost sight of her, but I still felt her presence, there somewhere in the room. I had a strange feeling that there was something familiar about her, but at the same time I knew that I had never seen her before. We listened to the music, but it seemed less important now. I couldn't get her out of my head and my friends kept encouraging me to go and talk to her, but I was just too shy.

The time passed and at the end of the evening, our milkshakes were getting quite warm. My chances of getting to know her were slipping away. I had to do something! I came up with the idea that we should leave early, before closing time, which was at 10:00 pm, and if she was still there at the table, I would talk to her on the way out—sort of casually. My friends agreed, but as the time approached to carry out the plan, I became more and more nervous. What should I say? What if she wouldn't talk to me? It would be SO embarrassing.

I walked past her table and I didn't even look at her, I simply didn't have the courage. I could have kicked myself!

Down in the street, I looked up at the building to see if I could catch a glimpse of her in one of the windows, and there she was, looking straight down at me. It was like a scene out of *Romeo and Juliet*. I was now determined to talk to her, having regained my confidence with the added distance between us.

'Let's wait till they close. She's bound to come down and then I'll walk over to her,' I said.

*

That evening, Mimi told me later, she had gone to Mælkepoppen with her two friends Annette and Jeannette to celebrate Annette's 15th birthday. It was their first time there too. They had arrived early and found a table in a good location from where they could keep an eye on the entry.

They enjoyed the loud music, one hit after another, much to their delight. Mimi sat between her two friends nursing a strawberry milkshake and played a game where she tried to catch the eyes of the boys that came in through the door to see how long she could keep their attention.

They hadn't been there long before Mimi turned to her friends and said, 'Look at that guy coming in now.'

'Which one?' asked Jeannette.

'The guy in the suede jacket, the dark-haired one between the two taller guys. They must be together, he keeps looking at me.' She started giggling and couldn't stop. The butterflies in her stomach weren't just fluttering, they were somersaulting from pure excitement.

The boys started walking towards their table, but she was too agitated to keep looking. Instead, she buried her face in the milkshake and they walked past and disappeared down the end of the long room, out of sight.

She spent the rest of the evening with her friends discussing what had happened; where *he* was, whether they had gone or not, and a sudden sadness came over her at the thought that he might have left without them noticing. Her friends tried to cheer her up, saying that he was bound to come back the same way, and if he was interested, he would surely come and talk to her, but nothing happened.

Then suddenly, he was right there, brushing past her table on the way out. She watched his back disappear through the door, and the same sadness she had felt earlier came over her again. The joy and excitement of being there had all disappeared.

'Look down there,' Jeannette said. She had spotted him standing on the opposite side of the street with his two friends. Mimi looked down and caught him looking back up at her with his dark eyes. His friends were goading him and laughing. Suddenly, she felt scared and withdrew quickly from the window. What if he was up to no good? She looked down again. They were still there, obviously waiting.

It was getting late, the place was closing down, and they had to leave. Conflicting thoughts raced through her mind. On the one hand, she was excited that he was still there, but on the other she was scared. In the end, the three girls went down the stairs and hurried away towards Rådhuspladsen, where the lights shone brightly.

*

I watched her disappear into the crowd, wedged safely between her two friends. I had planned to go over and talk to her when they came down, but when she finally appeared it was all too difficult. The courage I had felt just before had disappeared, and despite my friends urging me on, I held back.

But something must have switched inside of me, for suddenly I found myself running down the street, heart pounding. *I couldn't let her go, I just couldn't!* As if she had sensed my approach, she turned towards me inquisitively. Gently, I laid my hand on her shoulder and asked awkwardly, 'Hi, can I take you home?'

She must have been quite surprised. After all, it was not the first thing you would say to a person that you hadn't met before, but I was by myself and she was with her two friends, so in some way she must have felt safe.

'You can walk with us to Rådhuspladsen. We're catching a bus from there,' she said firmly.

After that, we didn't talk much. The girls walked in front of us, whispering and giggling, and I felt quite silly walking there without saying anything. What was I letting myself in for?

'Where are you going?' I asked to break the silence.

'Østerbro,' she said hesitantly.

'Oh good, I'm going the same way, so we can catch the bus together,' I lied. I lived in the opposite direction and I didn't know where the journey would end or how I would get home.

We crossed the square to the bus stop and it turned out that one of her friends had to catch a train from

Hovedbanegården, so they said goodbye to each other and the three of us were left behind. 'Where do you live?' Mimi asked suspiciously.

I had to think of something quickly. 'Near Trianglen,' I replied. I knew the place, because it was near the stadium where I used to go skating in winter time. She looked sweet in her duffle coat with the collar turned up over her ears for protection against the chill. How stupid I was, lying to her. I wondered what she would say if she found out.

There weren't many people on the bus. We sat at a safe distance from each other and talked about Mælkepoppen, the music we had heard, our likes and dislikes, whether we had been there before, and such things. She spoke with an unfamiliar accent that indicated Danish wasn't her first language. I tried to stay cool, while in reality I could barely control the feelings that overwhelmed me whenever I looked at her.

'What's your name?' I asked after some time.

'Marietta,' she answered, 'but my friends call me Mimi, and my sister's name is Jeannette.'

'My name is Viggo, can I call you Mimi?'

She smiled, which I took for a yes. I wondered how it could be that two people who appeared so different could be sisters. It wasn't just the accent that was different, but also her frizzy hair that she tried to keep in check with a ponytail, and which was in stark contrast to Jeannette's straight hair. When I asked her about it, she told me that her parents were divorced and she was visiting her sister who lived with her father. She herself lived in Glostrup, with her mother. It didn't explain the accent or the fact that they didn't look alike, but I didn't press the point.

We passed the lakes and the girls stood up, ready to get off at the next stop. I couldn't let them go just like that, so I asked if I could walk with them to the door where they lived. They agreed, but wanted to know where I lived. 'Oh, just a couple of stops ahead,' I said, 'I can walk home afterwards.' Lie upon lie, but I couldn't think of anything else to say.

We stopped at the door and neither of us wanted to say goodbye, so I asked if I could come up with them and stay for a little while. Jeannette seemed worried, but Mimi was keen. In the end they agreed, but Jeannette said that I couldn't stay long. Their dad wasn't home but would come later and they weren't allowed to bring anyone home. I couldn't believe my luck! We talked late into the night, and as I had expected, they weren't sisters at all. Mimi told me that she was Hungarian and that she had fled Hungary with her family during the 1956 revolution. Her parents were divorced and had both remarried, and they had all fled to Denmark together.

It was way past midnight, and I had to get home. I asked Mimi if we could meet again or if I could visit her at her mother's place.

'I'm Jewish,' she said, as if warning me off any further involvement.

'So what?' I replied. It didn't make any difference to me. I wanted to see her again.

'How many girlfriends do you have?' she probed.

'Well ... only one,' I said.

She told me that she didn't want to see me if I had another girlfriend.

I promised that I would finish the relationship with my girlfriend and we agreed I should go to her place the following Friday. We said goodbye in the doorway. She was so sweet and innocent, and any doubts that I had dissolved in a warm and tender kiss.

It was a long way home to Frederiksberg where I lived. There were no buses at that time of the night, so I walked along the edge of the lakes. The moon shone brightly in the cool clear night. I looked at the swans swimming so peacefully on the water. It seemed that I had never seen anything so serene and beautiful before. I didn't want the night to end.

In my mind, I went over what had happened. One thing had led to the next, as if it was meant to be. But now by myself, I began to have second thoughts. Was it possible to love two people at the same time? What about my promise? Could I lie to Mimi and pretend that I had broken up with my girlfriend? How should I break up with her, what should I say to her? Could I just drop her like that?

Joy was my first girlfriend; she was in a class below me at school. We had exchanged glances when we chanced upon each other at recess. Jan had been the go-between with messages until we finally met up. She lived nearby, and we would often see each other at her place after school. Now, I tried to avoid her in the schoolyard. It was not until Thursday, the day before I was to see Mimi, that I finally called her. But even as we were speaking, I couldn't tell her and instead suggested I'd go over to her place as usual. I wanted to tell her face to face. But when I arrived, I pretended that all was normal. I suggested we go for a walk, well aware that I was only prolonging the agony. It would be the last time we would walk together like this and an immense sense of loss came over me when I finally told her. She tried to stay calm, but couldn't hide her feelings. Tears rolled down her soft cheeks. I told her that I still loved her, but it only made things worse.

CHAPTER 11

'Oh, that's so sweet! And it's really well written, Viggo!' Abby is impressed. We chat for a little longer, and then she leaves. Listening to her reading Viggo's account again about how we met takes me back.

*

I'd certainly had a lot of crushes by the time I was 15, despite the fact that I used to have frequent physical fights with boys in the playground when I was younger, and had acquired quite a reputation.

Just a few years earlier, boys used to cross the road when they saw me coming. I told Lili about it. She said that I had to stop beating up boys if I wanted a boyfriend, and it made sense. Soon after, I started dance lessons and my partner was a boy from another school who had not heard about my reputation. We liked each other and he sometimes cycled over to my place to see me around the time Pista died. Years later, I heard that the association with me had earnt him the nickname 'the Hungarian' ever after our little romance. Poor boy!

Although 'the Hungarian' was sweet and our innocent summer crush and kisses were heartfelt, meeting Viggo a year later at the Mælkepoppen was so very different, so grown up! I spent the next week talking with my friends about him. Would he or wouldn't he come as promised? All week, every minute of the day, I was thinking about it, and discussing whether my friends thought he would keep his promise. 'I don't know,' they would reply, and 'What did he say?' 'Oh, yes, he is sure to come,' etc. etc., at school, at home, the whole time. I felt an enormous painful suspense because I didn't know whether he would come or not. I was in such turmoil about it all.

Finally it was Friday, the day he had promised to come, and the agony of waiting was almost unbearable. I went to look out the window over and over again, excited and scared at the same time. Would I still feel the same way as when we had met? A week was a long time. Was he a bad tough boy like other boys I had seen, the ones who wore leather jackets and went by the name of 'leatherjackets' in Danish? Would he harm me? He had seemed all right. Now, it was raining. Would he still come when it was raining? Finally, I just stayed by the window, sitting on the windowsill and looking down from my room on the second floor. Nothing was happening, nothing was happening … nothing was happening … and then suddenly, I saw a moped rider stop below. I didn't know how he would arrive, but there was this person on a moped and I thought that perhaps it was he, and I am certain that my heart was beating violently and my stomach was lurching and I hardly knew what to do with myself.

My doubts about the whole thing dissolved at the sight and sound of the moped approaching. And there he was, parking the vehicle below, wearing the same leather jacket as the previous night along with a black crash helmet. The helmet glistened in the soft, cold rain. He disappeared out of sight at the entrance to the stairwell. My excitement was indescribable. I blushed. My heart raced. My stomach was flip-flopping, and my mouth felt dry.

Then the doorbell rang. I opened the door and he was standing there in front of me on the doormat in the open doorway. He looked at me from under his wet hair, shyly and questioningly. Water was dripping from his jacket, his pants, and from the helmet in his left hand, and any doubts I had had before about his character disappeared. He was the same shy boy who had chased after me down Strøget only a week before.

'Hi,' I said. He looked a little different because his hair was squashed from the helmet and he seemed so ... foreign. I knew everyone, well almost everyone, in the community where I lived, and he was so foreign, this person, this strange person in the doorway, and he had come to see me all the way from Copenhagen, and I thought it was so exciting and adult-like.

Viggo had bought the moped off a friend of a friend. It had been parked in the bicycle shed where he lived for a long time and he had fallen in love with it. And then there was this thing, this coming of age, as one turned 16, when you were allowed to ride a moped. He didn't have much money. His earnings came from delivering milk for a delicatessen in the morning before school, so he had saved and saved and then bought this bike. With his newfound freedom, he could ride wherever he wanted, and Glostrup, where I lived, was a long way away, a newly built area with three-storey buildings, very modern compared with where he lived in an old building at Frederiksberg, almost in the centre of Copenhagen.

He was wearing layers of clothes because it was very cold to ride in November, particularly cold for his fingers. Viggo had been concerned about it all, about how he would be received, whether I still had feelings for him, so when he rang the bell, he was very nervous and then I opened the door ... and just smiled at him. I was wearing a woollen dress, he recalled, and he thought I looked so lovely as I was standing there, in the doorway and smiling at him. At the time, the Danish population was homogenous, and he thought that I looked so exotic. There were strange food smells wafting from the doorway, and he found it exciting that I was Hungarian.

My bat mitzvah confirmation was behind me, the Jewish rite of passage, and this had given me the confidence before he arrived to ask whether Viggo could visit me. My mother and stepfather were very strict, much more so than Danish parents, and I was anxious about asking, but they gave their permission. I invited him into my room and closed the door, and we were alone for the first time. We sat in awkward silence next to each other on the sofa, which doubled as my bed by night. He looked around my room, which was decorated with posters of The Beatles and all kinds of memorabilia, and compared it to his own room, which was a simpler, more functional space, a room he had taken full possession of when his older sisters had moved out.

On this first date, we just sat there gazing into each other's eyes. I had never before had a boy in my room who was not somehow connected to the family or to my parents' friends. By and by we picked up the conversation where we had left off the week before and I asked him whether he had broken off with his girlfriend. He told me that he had. We then talked a bit about school and I was impressed that he was in the grade above me, and a year older. But most of the time we just locked eyes in a series of breathless eternities. All the while I could tell he was thinking of kissing me, and I was longing for that tender kiss we had exchanged in the doorway on the night we met. I attempted to speak in a normal tone of voice, while secretly drowning in his velvet-brown gaze. By the time his wet clothes dried out near the radiator, it was time for him to leave, so we agreed that we would see each other again the following Friday after school.

Many such dates followed. It was amazing, the feelings we shared. Viggo would brave the snow, sleet, and cold rain during November and December to come and see me. He would be wet through, despite his best efforts to stay dry, and would use half the time standing in front of the radiator, drying his pants. Then we would sit on the sofa next to each other, holding hands and talking about our dreams and aspirations, what we thought our future lives would be like. Some evenings I had to babysit next door and he would join me, and my parents did not know he was there with me. It was very naughty. The neighbours had an L-shaped lounge and I would lie on my stomach on one side and he would lie on the other so we were facing each other, gazing into each other's eyes for hours, while pretending it was our own little baby we were looking after. It was so lovely. We didn't have to say much. There was a sense of stillness and peace between us.

Viggo knew that I had fled from Hungary and wanted to take care of me. He thought he could help me just by us being together. He told me later that he thought I seemed so innocent. I always had a wide, ready smile, but my eyes were sad, there was something very sad about me. He thought perhaps this was because my parents had divorced and I was a refugee. Either way, he didn't think I was happy, just pretending, always smiling and grinning. All he wanted to do was hold me, protect me, put his arms around me, but it was very scary because we didn't really know each other, so we just looked into each other's eyes. Sometimes, we listened to music, held hands, and snuck a kiss in before he left. Then, we'd count the days until we could see each other again.

On occasions when the weather allowed it, we would go ice skating hand in hand at the local frozen pond, trying to avoid the other skaters, taking turns pushing each other around. Sometimes he would help me with my math homework, or I would play my guitar and sing for him, or we would play records on my record player. But after just four weeks of 'going steady', I became worried that he might not love me as much as I loved him and that he might break up with me. I considered whether I should get in first, but then remembered his lips and kisses and sweet expressions, and decided with a quavering heart to dare to continue the relationship.

One night, he came with me to an end-of-term school party arranged for my class. I was so proud that he was my boyfriend, and I knew my classmates were watching us as we danced with each other all night. Even though I urged him to dance with my girlfriends, he only wanted to dance jive with me, although he secretly thought that I was not very skilled at dancing.

Viggo invited me to a New Year's Eve party at his friend Junker's place and for the first time I was allowed to stay out until 11 o'clock, when my stepfather would pick me up. During the night, Junker played his new Beatles' LP, *A Hard Day's Night* over and over. As we danced cheek to cheek, Viggo whispered in my ear, 'I love you, and I will love you forever.' It wasn't a thing he would have said lightly. It was like a seal, a lifelong commitment that could never be broken. When it was time for me to leave, he followed me downstairs. My stepfather was already waiting to pick me up.

I left with his tender words in my heart and got into the freezing petrol-smelling Skoda to ride home with my disapproving, cold, and hostile stepfather. Viggo waved as we drove off. There was an uncomfortable silence all the way home. The only solace was those words still ringing in my ear. He loves me, I thought, hiding my joy behind an expressionless face. Viggo, in turn, went back to join his friends upstairs, fielding a lot of questions about where we had met and where my funny accent came from. He explained that he had met me at Mælkepoppen and we had been going out ever since. At midnight, New Year's greetings were passed around at the party with the clinking of several bottles of Danish beer. Then the celebration gradually died down. A new year had begun with love and its promise of new exciting experiences ahead.

*

A few weeks later, my mother came into my room and announced that we were moving to Australia. NO! I jumped up onto the windowsill. The window was open and I said that I was going to jump out. The ground looked a long way down from our second-storey apartment. It made me dizzy and frightened.

'I don't wanna go!'
'Are you crazy!' my mother shouted, alarmed.
'I won't go; I'm staying here with my father!'

'If you don't want to come with us, you'll have to ask your father if you can stay with him ' she said. 'I bet he won't have you!'

She was obviously upset. Her face turned very pale. I climbed down from the windowsill.

'If you decide not to come with me you can forget you had a mother,' she said, and walked out of my room.

My mother and stepfather wanted to try a new life in Australia. My stepfather, who had studied to be a violin virtuoso alongside Menuhin before catching typhoid while interned in a concentration camp during the Second World War, was now a migrant factory worker in Denmark. He had heard that success in Australia was there for the taking for anyone who was willing to work hard. Ever since arriving in Denmark, he and my mother had wanted to migrate to America or Australia and they had finally received approval from the Australian embassy. Besides, the move would put distance between them and my father, who was a constant thorn in their sides, couriering nasty messages through me about my upbringing, which they struggled to provide, while he himself lived a lavish and grandiose lifestyle.

Viggo was crushed and shattered when I told him. He couldn't understand it at all, and kept searching for solutions. It felt like a disaster to him, a devastating event, as if the earth had moved beneath him. How could my parents make a decision like that without even thinking about us, about our feelings? Didn't our opinions count?

The following Wednesday, I received a letter from him. I wondered why he had written, especially as we had arranged for him to visit me on the Friday. I tore open the envelope and read, 'Dear Mimi! I've met another girl and won't be seeing you again.'

Viggo later described that letter as the 'cruellest and most cold-blooded' letter he had ever written. He'd felt he had to harden his soul to cope with the grief of losing me. He couldn't bear the thought of me leaving, couldn't stand the thought of saying goodbye to me at a train station or however I was going to leave. So he thought it would be best to break it off, because the more he saw me, the more he wanted to be with me and the worse it would be to see me go. He thought, 'If I break it off, then maybe it won't be so painful,' but it *was* painful for him during the weeks when he knew I was still in Denmark. He felt there was no meaning in life anymore.

Sleepless nights followed and several times he visited Mælkepoppen to see if he could catch a glimpse of me. Maybe he could talk to me and it would be like the old days and everything would be fine. But when he and his friend Jan did eventually see me there, it was too painful, so he pretended not to see me. Jan encouraged him to go and talk to me but it didn't happen. His need to protect himself won out. He couldn't handle that I was going to leave, he couldn't even imagine it. Yet the whole time, he could only think about me.

Then the time came for me to leave. He thought I could have chosen to stay. He became pretty wild after that, having one girlfriend after another, but nothing felt right. He thought he would never see me again but kept thinking about me.

*

We had only gone steady for about two months and our love was much too premature. I was 15 and he was 16. We were so young but our feelings for each other were overwhelming. After considering breaking up with Viggo myself because I had worried that he might break up with me first, I couldn't believe it when he wrote that letter saying he had met another girl and no longer wanted to see me. It didn't make sense, and I was devastated. I was in agony, upset all the time, heartbroken. We had had a beautiful New Year's Eve together, taking a walk away from the party, watching the fireworks light up the sky above our heads, our hands firmly clasped in each other's against the cold. The frost had glittered on the ground. We'd had a playful snowball fight, with red cheeks and noses, and laughter. And back at the party amidst the noise and dancing teens, he had kissed me and whispered that he loved me and would always love me.

However, he hadn't said it again since that night, which had made me feel insecure. And now it was over. I was terribly upset, sad and heavy inside, and my thoughts were constantly going around the why, why, WHY.

It took weeks before I began to go out and meet boys again, and as soon as they showed interest, I copied the same words Viggo had written to me and sent a letter to two or three boys before I felt I had got it out of my system. I still missed Viggo and I couldn't believe that he had broken up with me. I couldn't understand why. Everything had been fine, and then all of a sudden, it was over. I went to the Mælkepoppen a couple of times with some friends, all keyed up on the off-chance that I might meet him. After a few unsuccessful visits, one day he showed up with one of his tall friends and without the new girlfriend, but he did not approach me. When my friend and I walked past their table on our way out, Jan looked at me sadly and asked, 'How are you?' It was the worst thing he could have asked. I could hardly hold back my tears, just managed to say, 'I am fine' before rushing away. After that, I accepted that Viggo was no longer interested in me, and started going out with a sweet boy. We would cycle out to the Volden, lie in the tall grass and kiss, chat, and explore each other.

Then it was suddenly May, and I was on my way to a new life in Australia.

CHAPTER 12

A few months after Viggo's 'dear John' letter, we migrated across the world and arrived in Australia. I met Michael three weeks later on a blind date, arranged by his cousin whose father was an old Hungarian friend of my stepfather's. They had bumped into each other accidentally and rekindled their friendship. I was at their house in another room and could hear Michael approaching, talking with his cousin, laughing loudly, and occasionally clearing his throat in a cute way. When he entered, the whole atmosphere changed in the room. Before our date, he had dyed his hair jet-black and his eyes shone. Most importantly, he was both Jewish and Hungarian. His face resembled my father's. I didn't know it then, but he would become my first husband.

Shortly afterwards, a letter arrived for me from Denmark. I recognised the handwriting on the envelope, the same handwriting as on the dear John letter Viggo had sent me. My heart skipped a beat. It was a real surprise. Why would he write to me now? He wrote that he had asked my father for my address. He wanted me to know that what he had said in the letter was not true. There had never been another girl. It was something he had made up to defend himself against the pain of having to say goodbye to me when I left. He wrote that he still loved me and wanted to know how I felt about everything in my new life.

We corresponded for the next 18 months about developments in our lives. I told him about Michael and he wrote about the girls he went out with and what he had been doing. He often wrote that he missed me and hoped I would go back. He dreamt about becoming a pilot so he could fly to Australia one day to see me. He even attended training and examinations, but something was wrong with his ears, so he wasn't accepted.

At 16, it seemed to me that Sydney was stiff and formal and a hundred years behind Copenhagen's offerings, London's Carnaby Street, and Twiggy the model's miniskirts. There were few cafés, even fewer outdoor eateries. The city existed for business only, so it died shortly after 5 pm on weekdays and was almost deserted on weekends. The most exciting foods available were to be found in the one obligatory Chinese restaurant located in almost every suburb and country town, as well as a couple of Hungarian restaurants in Sydney's eastern suburbs.

I left school when we migrated to Australia because I was hopeless at mathematics and chemistry, so I couldn't study medicine, which had been my passion and profession of choice, and I had no plan B other than to become a good wife and mother. I got a job as a junior in the office at Jack Jeffrey's Motors in Rose Bay. I could walk to and from work from our flat in Wellington Street, Bondi, and earnt the princely sum of £7 a week. The job involved endless filing, making and serving tea for the owners, who were very particular about how the tea should be enjoyed, and going shopping at the local health food shop, particularly for honey to sweeten the tea and for freshly squeezed peanut butter. I obsessed about saving enough money to buy the gorgeous pink bikini displayed in a shop that I passed to and from work each day. Soon after I accomplished that goal, my mother and stepfather invited me to work at the new café they had bought in Bondi Junction. I left my mind-numbing job with relief, and my presence in the café proved to be a bit of an asset: I was young, lively, friendly, and flirtatious, and this brought in new customers—right up until an ugly incident a year later when my stepfather called me a slut during a heated discussion. I was no slut. At 17, I had only ever made love to Michael, who was my steady boyfriend. In utter outrage, I quit my job immediately.

A period of unemployment followed. I felt isolated and homesick, imagining myself walking along the beloved Danish concrete footpaths and longing for my old friends more each day. Outside, there was continuous torrential rain, mirroring how my heart felt. One day when I was alone at home during a period of unemployment, I almost turned on the gas for the gas heater. Taking my own life was by no means a new thought. I had often thought about it during my childhood and discussed it with Pista, and it was my go-to thought whenever I felt upset. But this time I frightened myself and thought, NO! Nothing is bad enough for that. Instead, I wrote to my father and asked him to buy me a ticket back to Denmark. It took a long time for the ticket to arrive. I had turned 18 by the time I was sitting on the plane.

While I waited to return to Denmark, I missed Viggo, Lili, and all my Danish friends, as I'd found it difficult to make friends in Australia. My life seemed purposeless. Michael was the only bright point but our relationship was volatile, as he frequently took liberties with me. Sometimes he would shout me down, and even physically hurt me during one of his rages. Then I would refuse to see him ever again, but somehow, he always persuaded me to forgive him. Although his boundary breaches were shocking to me, there was simultaneously something familiar about being treated this way. The abuse almost seemed to me a demonstration of how much he cared, an evidence of his love. But after 18 months of going steady, our relationship had grown a little stale. I was waiting for my return ticket to Denmark and with neither of us committed, we agreed to take a break.

I found a job as a waitress in a hotel where I met a dashing young waiter. We had a whirlwind romance and he asked me to marry him after two weeks. I was seriously toying with the idea, when Michael found out about it from my concerned mother, who had asked him for assistance, and one morning he turned up unexpectedly and convinced me to take a drive with him. During the drive he insisted that I break up with the waiter. I refused. He kept driving, and soon we were outside Sydney on the highway, despite my protestations. He wouldn't stop driving or take me home until I promised to quit both the job and the boyfriend. I was moved by Michael's impassioned behaviour and the level of his distress on learning about my infidelity. We both cried a lot. By the time we were back in Sydney, we had made up and I promised to stay faithful to him.

*

I had written to Viggo and told him that I was on my way home. When I arrived in Copenhagen I called him, and the next day he rode to my father's place on his new motorbike. Two and a half years had passed since we had first met. I opened the door in excited anticipation. It was like the old days, standing in the doorway and smiling at each other, except that we were both older. We looked into each other's eyes, but I felt nothing. In retrospect, I don't think I wanted to feel the same feelings for Viggo again. I had wondered how it would be to see him again, but it wasn't like before.

Perhaps it was because I had met Michael, who was gregarious and full of ideas. He had a car and attended university, and we could talk about all sorts of things, like philosophy and psychology. I had never met anyone I could talk with at that deep level, and I fell in love with that. When I was unemployed, I often accompanied Michael to his lectures at Sydney University, and later we discussed what we had learnt. Often, we would go for a midnight snack, buy a foot-long hot dog at Henry's drive-in, and eat it while listening to top 10 in Michael's car, or drive to the Cross and eat long soup at our favourite Chinese restaurant.

Viggo had always been quiet in comparison, really quiet. He and I had never had deep discussions, so that was a big difference. By the time we met up again, I'd experienced another significant relationship to compare him against, and it didn't feel the same as when I'd first met him. I had changed a lot; I was no longer the sweet innocent girl that Viggo remembered. I was a young adult now, but he still loved me, loved me perhaps even more than before.

I let him kiss me and invited him inside. My father greeted him and made him feel comfortable and accepted, while trying to find out what kind of a guy he was, this boy I had told him about. My father had an air of arrogance and success about him that he did not mind showing off. He asked Viggo, 'How do you like your Martini,' thereby signalling that he was willing to treat a 19-year-old like an adult. Viggo could have answered, 'Shaken, not stirred,' but that would have been inappropriate and besides, he was naturally very polite.

My stepmother Lili was the perfect hostess. She had prepared little snacks for us all to enjoy. This reception was in stark contrast to the frosty and suspicious one that Viggo had always experienced at my mother's and stepfather's home, a home where I was always made to feel, somehow, as if I had committed or was capable of committing a variety of bad things, and that I was a bad person.

When Viggo left, I agreed to meet him again in town and have lunch at Magasin du Nord, an upmarket department store at Kongens Nytorv. A few days later, we met up at Strøget and walked to Magasin du Nord, where we had my favourite open prawn sandwiches in the upstairs cafeteria. Then we went downstairs to buy a bottle of Scotch for my father, an errand I would often do for him when I was in town, because it was cheaper there than at his local grocer.

After a couple of weeks back in Denmark, I secured a position at an advertising agency. It was a job I enjoyed. I got on well with my young supervisor and we shared many laughs and some evening meals at her home with her little family. I was slowly settling into my new life back in Denmark.

One evening, Viggo's mother invited me for tea. She had prepared *frikadeller*, traditional Danish oval meatballs. After dinner we went to Viggo's room and listened to music. Another night soon after, Viggo and I went to a party. As the evening wore on, couple after couple made their way into the bathroom. When the bathroom became free, Viggo suggested that we should go in too. He draped someone's towel on the stone tiles and we lay down to make love, but it felt cheap and awful to be there on the floor, and I said I wanted to go back to the party. That was the only time we came close to making love.

Viggo took it for granted that I was his girlfriend now that I was back in Denmark, and this was reinforced by the reception he had received from my father and Lili, but it could not have been further from the truth. I was keeping up a constant correspondence with Michael, who had many plans for our future. In contrast, I had no idea whether Viggo had any plans, as he never talked about them with me. All I knew was that he was studying something, somewhere. And that he had brown eyes and beautiful soft lips.

While I was in Australia, Viggo had left school and accepted an electrical apprenticeship. Viggo's mother knew someone who was an engineer and Viggo thought it was an amazing profession. One of the entrance requirements was a trade. As it turned out, Viggo didn't like the trade or getting up at 5 o'clock in the morning, dragging cables through the mud. He also didn't like the people he worked with, whom he thought weren't very bright. Soon, he gave it up to attend night school in order to matriculate, studying and completing the course in two years instead of three. Because he wanted to be an engineer, it was very intense and he didn't have much time to go out.

I, on the other hand, was working, but my evenings and weekends were free and I had a lot of time on my hands. So, although I saw Viggo from time to time, I also started dating other boys. I had stayed faithful to Michael, as I had promised him before I left Australia.

It was an ill-conceived promise. Now that I was on the other side of the world, I soon reinterpreted 'faithful' as 'not going all the way'. I was back in

Denmark, free and young, wild and reckless, buffeted by the storm of my unplanned life, looking outside for the love that had never lived inside me, yearning to anchor my life to a special someone and finally belong. I was experimenting with relationships, enjoying the attention of the young men buzzing around me, carefully steering all conversations around to marriage. There was a lot of heavy petting going on, but I kept my promise to Michael.

Soon I was going out with four boys at the same time. One of them was my former boyfriend, 'the Hungarian' from my old dance classes. I carefully allocated a specific weekday to each boy. I was looking for someone to marry and had the boys lined up, one each day, playing the field. But Viggo, who thought he had a special relationship with me, arrived unannounced one day while another boy was visiting. It was an uncomfortable experience and neither of them knew what to do, eyeing each other off unhappily, while I watched on. Viggo ended up leaving, although he later said he should have stayed, he should have said, 'Bugger off' as he wanted to 'piss that guy off'. He ruminated over this episode, although he later thought it had been quite hilarious, with them both stubbornly waiting for the other to leave. He told me much later that he felt sidelined and could not understand why he was no longer the most important person for me, although we never discussed it. I was not the Mimi he'd known in 1964. I was a young adult, enjoying my female powers.

*

Life with my father and Lili was not what I had imagined back in Australia, right from my first day back. To welcome me home, they invited their friends from upstairs, a Hungarian architect and his wife. My father was drunk, and soon started to interrogate me in front of everyone about why I had wanted to come back. I made the mistake of telling them about being called a slut by my stepfather, and warned my father never to call me that. Next, he urged me to tell all. Was I still a virgin? I was shocked that he would ensnare me into such a humiliating situation in front of his friends. I had travelled non-stop for 36 hours across the world and was exhausted. It had been a very big step to take and all I wanted was warmth, love, and understanding.

Instead, my father sat comfortably back in his armchair like a king on a throne, expertly sloshing the ice in his whisky glass as if it was a sceptre, subjecting me to his embarrassing questioning and debasing my mother in the process. Why had she not kept an eye on me! This was the price I had to pay for his do-gooding, sending me a ticket home. After all, he had rescued me and he felt I owed him. I looked at Lili, hoping she would stop him, but she seemed to enjoy the spectacle and the guests were also clearly amused. I got up and left the room, sobbing in despair at how my longed-for reception in Denmark had worked out, with Lili running after me down the hall, scolding me that I was rude and ungrateful, demanding that I return.

My father clearly took my request never to call me a slut as a dare, and one morning soon afterwards he said it. Without a thought, I fell upon him like a wild, wounded animal and almost scratched one of his eyes out. I was extremely distraught about what I had done and what he had said, and immediately left home. I went to Lili's brother's place and explained the situation, asking him and his wife whether I could stay until I found alternative accommodation. They were very welcoming and said I could stay as long as I needed to. I immediately became sick with a cold from the stress and called work to tell them I would be away for a few days.

To my surprise, Lili's brother also decided that he was sick and stayed at home. This went on for a few days and the situation became increasingly uncomfortable as he tried to convince me the entire day to have sex with him. I was shocked. 'You're my stepmother's brother! You have a wife and a four-year old,' I pointed out. But none of this deterred him until his wife came home from work one day and shouted in no uncertain terms for me to get out. I could not believe what was happening to me, reeling from these cascading traumatic events. Fortunately I was able to stay with friends for a few days until I found accommodation in a boarding house on Amager owned by a sour old landlady. She was very controlling, often calling up to me from her landing, lecturing me about one of my apparent misdemeanours. Her many unreasonable rules got the better of me, so after a few weeks I found a newly built student accommodation in Herlev and finally felt safe again. The rent was expensive and I lived on a diet of black coffee for breakfast, a large spring roll for lunch, and a small head of cauliflower and Danish camembert for dinner.

Viggo helped with the move and as it was getting late, I agreed that he could stay the night. We undressed and lay naked in bed, soon falling asleep with our arms wrapped around each other. There was no sexual desire, just a feeling that this was so right, tender, complete, and peaceful, that it was where we both belonged. The next morning he got up briskly and went to the bathroom to wash. The sun was streaming into my little room through the bare curtain-less window and it was very light. The room still smelled of fresh paint and new wooden doors. We shared a black espresso for breakfast, made on my tiny espresso machine. Then I sat up behind him on his motorbike and he drove me to work. We rode silently, bathed in the warmth between us. Something had happened, something significant. We had seen each other at our most dishevelled, sleepy worst and yet it seemed it would be easy to slip into this kind of life together.

However, the thought frightened me. I didn't want to live with him, he was a threat to my worldliness and elusiveness. His warmth and demand for exclusivity threatened to clip my wings. His adoration was suffocating; I didn't know how I could live with that level of security and gentleness. It felt more comfortable to love someone who loved me less, someone I had to fight for, like Michael. I never knew where I was with him. He was often unpredictable, rude, rejecting, hurtful, and even violent. I was familiar with that kind of behaviour, reminiscent of my relationship with my four parents. In contrast, I had clearly conquered Viggo long before, and although I could sense his despair and his deep love, it was the wrong time for me. Being with him felt dull. I had already seen something more exciting that beckoned to me and although it was true that something special had happened between us, I resisted it, refused to feel it.

Our lives slipped further and further apart. One night we were both at Karusellen, a dance restaurant with live bands frequented by young people. I was there with a new boyfriend when I saw Viggo dancing with other girls. Neither of us acknowledged the other although we were both aware of each other's presence. Still, we saw each other on and off, when Viggo was free after studying and working and I wasn't busy with my social life. Over the next nine months, I received several marriage proposals and even Viggo and I discussed marriage, although he never said he wanted to marry me. He thought I was going to stay in Denmark but soon suspected that I was only visiting. By then, I had made up with my father in Hellerup and moved back home.

Then Viggo suddenly took off on a motorbike holiday to England with his friend Junker. He sent me a postcard from Carnegie Street, the fashion street of London at the time where everyone was wearing flared trousers. He wrote, 'I wish you were here,' and I stuck the postcard on the outside of the door to my loft room. The loft was essentially just a dark corridor with little rooms on each side for storage, but my father had refurbished his with proper walls and heating. The room was furnished and cosy. On a side table I kept a framed photo of Michael. When I'd been corresponding with Viggo from Australia, I had told him about an incident when Michael lost his temper, shoved me into a wall, and shouted at me. I remember how shocked I had been. I could not understand what I had done to enrage him so, and why he felt entitled to do that to me. He eventually apologised.

When Viggo saw the photo, he could not accept that I had it in my room, or that I could entertain the thought of continuing the relationship. He hated Michael, even though he'd never met him.

Of course, Viggo didn't know anything about Michael's background, how Michael had also fled Hungary as a child, or how his mother's family had all been exterminated during the Second World War. Michael's mother had never recovered from the loss of her family, even after she got married and had children. One day after school, Michael went home to find she had committed suicide. It was her third or fourth attempt, and on the previous occasions, he had managed to save her. His father then sent him away to boarding school. So much pain! I felt protective of him and curiously responsible somehow, so I forgave him again and again for his bad behaviours.

I continued corresponding with Michael while dating other boys, Viggo being just one of them. Viggo wondered where all the love we used to feel for each other had gone. He felt he couldn't offer me anything, couldn't suggest we get married. Besides, at 19 he was too young to marry without permission from the Danish queen. Whenever we were together, Viggo was either withdrawn or pouty or looking at me sadly, as if he was thinking, 'How could she do this to me?'

CHAPTER 13

My four boyfriends were gradually reduced to two—Leif and Niels—who had both asked me to marry them. Viggo often visited, sitting in a chair facing me, caressing me sadly and longingly with his soulful eyes. I decided that I preferred Niels and broke off with Leif, although the whole time I was still writing to Michael frequently. Michael wrote that he missed me badly. His aim was to get a job and save up for a ticket to Europe so he could join me, but the job fell through and he couldn't get another job, and he couldn't save up. Nevertheless, he was still planning to fly to England, or planning something or other. I didn't really know what his plans were, but he was always full of plans and promises, and they all sounded enticing.

Niels was a sweet boy and very keen. He romanced me, but I wasn't totally comfortable about considering his proposal. I did not really want to marry him, but he was attached to the idea and kept pressuring me to make a decision. On impulse I called Michael long distance from my father's apartment. It was lovely to hear his voice again. He said he could not afford to come to Denmark and asked whether I would return to Australia instead.

'Do you want to marry me?' I asked him.

'Yes,' he said.

I told him I would save up and return to Australia. When I finished that phone call, I felt really down, *really* depressed. There are certain moments you remember and that moment is imprinted in my mind. I felt a dread in my gut I had never felt before, as if I had done something very bad. I should have been elated, but a wave of sadness washed over me. I paced up and down, and then walked into the kitchen. From the kitchen window I could see the yard below. It was grey; everything looked grey and my heart sank, and the thought of the marriage to Michael felt like a sentence. But I didn't listen to myself. I didn't know why I had to do it, but I was driven. So I started to save for my return, and Michael's thick letters to me were filled with excitement. He was keen to get married. He certainly didn't have anything to offer me, although it was Viggo who had said he didn't have anything to offer. Michael had just said yes, he wanted to marry me, and that was all the offer I needed.

Despite the dread, there was a feeling of inevitability, of being propelled forward by something much larger than myself. I felt compelled to marry Michael. I had a maternal need to protect him, and there was also a sense of our unwritten pact, of the two of us against an unfair world. But most importantly there was a commitment somewhere deep inside me to give birth to Jewish children. My mother had been a prisoner in Auschwitz, where her parents and most of her extended family had been exterminated. The same happened to my father's parents and most of his extended family, although he himself had been interred in a Hungarian work camp, which apparently was not much of an improvement on concentration camps. He never talked about his traumatic experiences there, or about his life before the war. So I felt responsible to do my part in regenerating the devastated Jewish population, the result of the Holocaust.

Although I was born four years after the end of the war, I had felt its effects all my life. I had always longed for the grandmothers I never had. As a small child I had always wished I could hide my little face and cry into their big breasts and be comforted, unconditionally, in a grandmotherly way. Although I had never known them, I had always felt the emptiness left behind by my many family members who had died in the gas chambers or been gunned down. I had always felt lonely, felt like the sad remnants of my family, the few who had somehow survived. Perhaps that was why my eyes were always sad despite my outward smile.

My motivation to marry at the young age of 18 also had its history in my early childhood. I came into the world as a result of a doctor's assessment of my mother's depression following World War II. The doctor hypothesised that it would do her good to have a child. A child would give her hope and provide her with a future and a purpose. So she followed the doctor's advice, but had little to give me.

I learnt to curb my need for her love, and instead looked for romantic love to fill the void from an early age. Already at the age of six, the only threat that helped me give up sucking my thumb, after several other measures had failed, was my father's prediction that if I sucked my thumb the boys would not dance with me. By that time I had experienced the love of several little boys at preschool. They chased me and sprayed me with cheap perfume as part of a Hungarian Easter tradition. The preschool teachers' smiling approval (and perhaps that of my parents) would have conveyed the importance of the boys' interest in me. Encouraged, I decided at the age of six to give up my self-soothing behaviour and wait for all my emotional needs to be provided by a male.

Once Upon a Love

*

I told Niels I couldn't see him anymore, and he was heartbroken. But my path was now set. Viggo also took it badly. He was devastated that I was leaving. Hadn't we slept together—albeit platonically? Didn't we love each other? How could I leave? Yet he continued to visit me, and all I felt was disdain that verged on disgust at his morose clinginess. I'm not sure why. Perhaps it was how my mother had felt about me when I was small. I told him that if it didn't turn out the way I felt it should with Michael, I would come back and marry him. There I was, leaving a second time, like a wild bird. He couldn't cage me in, I had to fly away and do what I had to do. This time, I could have chosen to stay in Denmark—but I didn't.

He said he might take his own life. This concerned me so much that I wrote to my mother about it. She wrote back advising me not to stay with someone out of fear of their committing suicide. I trusted her advice because I knew that she had stayed with my stepfather for exactly that reason and had frequently been unhappy in the relationship.

A short time after I made my decision to return to Australia, Viggo and I were invited to a party in Nord Sjælland. We rode up there on the motorbike. It was not what we had expected. People were smoking dope and having sex. As it was late, we slept there but returned in the rain the next morning. The road was slippery and the motorbike skidded and tipped over. Viggo was shielded by the motorbike but I wasn't. He took me to the hospital where they cleaned out the grit from the asphalt and bandaged me up. I called home and Lili answered the phone.

'There's no need to worry, we've just had a little accident and I've grazed my legs but I'm okay,' I told her.

My father was alarmed at the sight of me when we arrived back home. My foot was in bandages and I was limping around. He was appalled that I had travelled on the bike with Viggo, who was very apologetic and sat down to try and explain what had happened. He asked them to forgive him, and they accepted his explanation.

Despite no apparent damage to my bones, I was unable to walk for weeks. I called work, told them I would not be back, and spent the remaining time in Denmark outstretched on the sofa, reading Tolstoy's *War and Peace*. Viggo visited frequently during this period, feeling very sad and guilty about the whole thing. Secretly, he hoped that the accident would prevent me from returning to Australia, but I had made up my mind.

Four years after we first met, Viggo saw me off at Central Station in Copenhagen. I was still wearing slippers but I could at least walk.

*

Viggo kept writing to me after I married Michael. I thought it best not to reply, and eventually the letters came less frequently. Then, after a long pause, a final letter came. I opened it up. A photo fell out of the letter, of Viggo in Italy. He wrote that he had met someone, and asked if I was sure that I wanted to stay with Michael.

I did not respond. Eight years passed.

CHAPTER 14

Now, after a holiday intended to save our marriage, Michael and I were on a plane back to Australia with the children, each passing hour separating me more from Denmark and Viggo.

Michael and I were carefully polite to each other, courteous strangers supervising our two small children whose pent-up energy was expended crawling on the dirty floors of each airport all the way back to Sydney.

My mother was aware of my troubled marriage. She knew that Michael was an absent husband both physically and emotionally. She did not know, however, that he could also be violent and abusive, once breaking a cup over my head while I cried inconsolably; it was a wedding present. She didn't know either about the time he had slammed on the brakes during our honeymoon, screaming at me to get out of the car on the highway and then leaving me standing there. She had not seen the holes he kicked in doors, or that he argued about the way I parented in front of the children during the rare times when he was at home.

She was aware that we were working on our relationship because before going to Denmark, I had asked her to look after the children when Michael and I took a weekend away at the suggestion of my counsellor. That was our first weekend away, and the first time she had looked after the children since they were born—as she had often told me, I had wanted the children so I should look after them.

When we returned from our overseas trip, I visited her and told her about Viggo. She listened and finally asked, 'What are you going to do?'

I said I intended to continue with my marriage, even though my marriage to Michael had ended on the second night of our return. He had taken me in his arms to make love, but we both failed through a lack of love for each other. It was no longer working for me; not after Viggo. It was sad that this had to happen after we had children. I should have left him before they were born. There had certainly been enough reasons to do so.

We had put our belongings in storage while we were away and, on our return, stayed with Michael's father until we found a house to rent. His father had always asked us to move in with him but I had refused, fearing that I would eventually have to become his carer. I didn't want that responsibility and was adamant that this would be a short stay, so I was relieved when we found a house.

On the morning of the move, Michael announced that he had to attend a job interview. Again, there I was doing the marriage on my own, this time organising the removalists as well as our small children. Lunchtime came and went. Michael had left me no money, so I had no food to give the children. Even if I'd had the money, I could not have left the removalists and gone shopping. While I was in the middle of washing up all the stored crockery and cutlery, anxiously wondering how I was going to pay the removalists, Michael walked in casually, chewing on a ham and tomato sandwich.

He paid the removalists and walked into the kitchen, chomping on the sandwich, oblivious to the fact that neither the children nor I had eaten. He saw me washing up at the sink. 'Give me a glass of water, please?' he said.

'Sure,' I replied as I filled a freshly cleaned glass with water from the tap. I threw the water at him along with the glass. He dropped to the floor, moaning and holding his head where the glass had shattered and made him bleed. I swore loudly, helped him up, and bundled him and the frightened children into the car. At the hospital, he was asked whether he wanted to press charges. He declined. After that, we slept in separate bedrooms.

Our marriage irrevocably ended the day we moved into the house that should have framed our future.

My pain at missing Viggo was unbearable and I began to self-medicate with alcohol. Drinking became a habit. I daydreamt of him whenever my attention was not taken up by the children, or by the early childhood studies I had enrolled in soon after our return. I missed him so much, my body ached for him. I wrote him many letters, long, handwritten letters. Some were filled with descriptions of my pain. Others were deliberately superficial, casual and cheerful, telling him about my daily life and omitting my tortured state. I made no mention of how much I loved and missed him.

I sent none of those letters, ripping them up. I couldn't tell him how often I thought about him, how much he meant to me. It would have scared him away even further. Anyway, our situation was hopeless. I was on the other side of the world, married with two children.

Three months after our return to Australia and after all those long letters I had never sent, I was at the newsagent's when I spotted a postcard of the Opera House, famously designed by another Danish architect. Spontaneously, I bought it and wrote, 'This is your house,' signing it 'Your Mimi'. I hoped that the simple message would convey to him how much I missed him, how much he meant to me, and that his future was with me. This time, I posted it and then waited. I worked out that if he wrote back straightaway, I could expect his response in about 10 days. After the eighth day, I ran to the post box each morning with a pounding heart. But no letter came and I grew more and more despondent with each passing day.

In the meantime, my mother and stepfather had gone on holiday to Fiji for two weeks. When they returned, I visited with the children. There, my mother handed me a letter addressed to me. It had arrived while they were away. It was from *him*, it was his handwriting. I was ecstatic. I thought, 'He loves me, he loves me after all, he can't live without me!' I looked at the date on the envelope. He had sent it at exactly the same time as I had sent my postcard. They had crossed the world simultaneously, on the same day, after three months of torturous silence …

We began a tentative, careful, irregular correspondence, with sometimes weeks or months between letters. It was a difficult dance, maintaining this precarious connection without demands or expectations. Despite our affair and our feelings for each other, we did not want to make any claims on each other or make any promises. Viggo had separated, was back working full time, and was trying to settle into the house he had moved to after leaving his marital home. He had painted it and moved the furniture around and invited people to dinner, trying to adjust to living alone in a house that was too large for him.

We were both busy. He was working, and I had very little spare time between attending college, doing assignments, commuting, and parenting two small children. But I was never too busy for his letters, which I awaited each day. When one arrived, I feverishly examined each word for meaning, for news about developments in his life that were directly linked to our love, for signs between the lines that he still loved me.

Weeks and months passed. I left Michael. Both Viggo and I applied for divorces, although we only casually mentioned these events in our letters. I missed Viggo dreadfully and tried to go out with other men, but this only made my longing more painful. No one could fill the void he had left in my heart, and it seemed inevitable that I had to eventually be with him. All those years before, when our eyes had first met, it was as if two exact halves had recognised each other. From that moment, we were fated to be together.

At that time, however, it was too soon. We were too young and immature to understand and surrender to such deep and complex emotions. There were obvious reasons that we had chosen our first partners. They had shaped our future professions and we had needed their guidance. There was my non-negotiable need to bear Jewish children. I had been determined to marry early but had not been ready for the kind of relationship that I could have had with Viggo. With my deep fear of commitment, I'd always had one foot and half of my heart out the door, lest I become entrapped and hurt, remembering my father's warning not to be like other women.

When I'd married Michael, my expectations for a long-term marriage were low. Family members wondered whether the marriage was going to last because we were so young, and I would respond jokingly that it was better to have loved for two years than not at all. Now, having borne my Jewish children and with both Viggo's and my professions clarified, we were again confronted by our overwhelming love for each other, embellished by irresistible sexual desire. This time, we felt it equally and longed for a deep, passionate, and committed relationship. Despite the challenges we would have to overcome—living in separate countries, my children—there was a magnetic pull towards a life that we simply had to share.

Even so, our correspondence remained patchy. Each time Viggo wrote, I refrained from writing back immediately, not wanting to appear too needy. He too was slow to respond. Then one day, about a year after I returned to Australia, I received one of his letters. I touched the envelope tenderly, knowing he would have touched it. I tried to detect his Viggo-scent as I opened up the folded pages. His letters always caused me a mixture of dread and expectation. Would his letter include plans that did not include me? Had he met another woman? Did he still love me?

Yes, he must, because he wrote that he had been running along the Furesøen lake, thinking about me and visualising marrying me. My heart jumped as I read on. He had been running along a straight, well-worn, wide pathway with tall trees that somehow seemed to him to resemble a cathedral. He felt as if he was in a church; it was an almost spiritual experience. Then he had sat on the lawn beside the path and thought about his whole life, what he was doing, and where he was going. While sitting there, he had picked some blades of grass and plaited them into a ring. He wrote that his relationship with me was like a spiritual journey because that was what it was like when you really loved someone. My eyes left the page as something slipped into my lap.

It was the grass ring, which had fallen out when I unfolded his letter.

CHAPTER 15

Viggo is stirring in the bed beside me as I glance at my wedding ring. Our rings were crafted by a jeweller who designed them to resemble the plaited grass ring Viggo sent me years before. The plaiting was a metaphor for our entangled relationship, going into and out of each other's lives.

After so many years, our wedding rings have become worn and polished, a few sharp corners knocked off along the way, just like those traits of ours that were damaging to our relationship.

Viggo stirs again, and I look up from my reverie.

'Hello, darling, did you have a nice sleep?'

'Did I sleep? What's the time?'

He spends a lot of time sleeping now. We are quiet for a while.

'Can I ask you a question? Are you afraid of dying, Treasure? Would you like to speak with a counsellor?'

'Yeah, perhaps it would be a good idea.'

The palliative care unit's counsellor arrives in the early afternoon.

I vacate my chair near the window and move to the other side of the bed, so she can sit near him. She bends over close to him, as he can only speak softly now. She asks him what he would like to talk about, and they chat for a while. Then she asks about his earliest experience of death.

'The death monster, I saw it on television! I was very young. I must have been … it was in '56, so I must have been eight years old. I remember that my mother worked in, ah, I can't remember what that street was called, in … Ranzausgade. Anyway, it was a few streets away from where we lived and she used to cycle to work. She worked in a delicatessen, and her boss had invited all his staff and their families to his home for dinner to raise money for the Hungarian aid campaign. He was well off and had a TV, so we were going to watch the program about the fundraising, and donate to the campaign.

'It was terrible. I saw all these people who had been shot, and tanks driving around the streets, and I thought it was just dreadful. I wanted to help those people so much, but I couldn't. It was shocking.'

There is silence; Viggo closes his eyes for a minute before going on.

'I remember the black-and-white TV, which was at one end of the room and at the opposite end, a window faced the street. People were gathered around the table, which was laden with food from the delicatessen that my mother's employer had provided for the occasion. He then sent a hat around the table and everyone placed notes in there for the aid campaign. Loud noises came from the TV. I asked what was happening. It looked like people were getting shot at. They said it was a revolution in Hungary. There were young Hungarian revolutionaries standing and waving a flag on top of a tank. There were dead people lying on the ground. It was the first time I had ever seen death close up. Some people were pleading for their lives as a big tank approached them. Others were hiding in doorways and on porches, and they were terrified.'

Viggo repeats the word 'death monster' over and over. He becomes agitated, his speech increasingly garbled. The counsellor thanks him and suggests that he should rest. Then she motions to me that she will come back later. Viggo closes his eyes and I am left to my own memories of the revolution.

*

The revolution started in 1956, the year that I turned seven. Almost right up to that time I had spent my young life in virtual isolation in our studio apartment with my nanny, whom I called Anyus (Mum is *Anyu* in Hungarian, but I had added an 's').

My father was over-protective as a result of his experiences during World War II, which had ended a few years before I was born. He was terrified that something would happen to me. There were still many fascists around who hated Jews, so I was always watched over and mostly kept within four walls. Unfortunately, this shuttered early childhood existence was not conducive to mental health, and my father only agreed to enrol me in preschool on the advice of the consulting psychologist they took me to see when I began experiencing symptoms of depersonalisation. My joy at this welcome escape to preschool and playmates was short-lived, however, because of the many viruses I caught as soon as I was exposed to other children. While I continued attending preschool, I still lived a rather cloistered existence because of my many absences.

At that time in Hungary, school started at six and so I eventually had to leave preschool, my little friends, and my lovely preschool teacher. Even Anyus was no longer needed during the day, so my mother looked for another carer who could just take me to school and pick me up in the afternoon. She found an old retired schoolmarm and took me along for the interview, hissing for me to behave with a warning look flashing in her brown eyes as she rang the doorbell. I took an instant dislike to the schoolmarm, but sat quietly at a highly polished table next to my mother, taking in the chandeliers and the high windows, listening to their conversation. The schoolmarm's grey hair was drawn into a tight bun at the back of her head and she looked very strict, not at all kind like my gentle Anyus. I noticed how she tried to impress and charm my mother, who was apparently oblivious to the woman's insincerity, and perhaps a little desperate. I heard my mother assuring her that I was a very good child.

Surprised, I looked up at her face, certain that she was lying to convince the old schoolmarm to take the job. My mother had never given *me* the impression that I was good. I always seemed to be an irritant to her, too wilful, too needy, and too lively. She often told me off. She often seemed annoyed with me. When I occasionally reached up to hold her hand at the tram stop, I'd burn my palm on her lit cigarette, which she invariably held in the hand closest to me. When she brushed my hair in the mornings, she yanked the brush angrily through my tight curls and banged the bristles into my scalp when I writhed around in pain.

One day when she was crying during a Balaton Lake family holiday, I asked her if she was crying because I had been naughty, even though I somehow knew that her despair had to do with my father. She nodded in agreement, her wet face in her hands. I said I was sorry and she allowed me to hug her. That was the first time I had felt like a protector, and we sat there together and cried for a long time.

Although my mother tolerated me, I knew that she thought I was a difficult and bad child. Thus, I watched the interesting exchange: my mother, ignoring the schoolmarm's insincerity, and the schoolmarm, pretending to believe that I was a good child and promptly accepting the position my mother offered her. From then on, either she or her husband picked me up from school, and I stayed in the apartment with the chandeliers and high windows until one of my parents came to collect me.

Then, after what seemed like a very short while, the schoolmarm announced that I had to stay overnight as well. I didn't know why, or for how long. Unbeknown to me, my parents had split up and entered new relationships. My mother had moved out of our studio apartment to live with the man who would become my stepfather. My father stayed in our apartment and Lili moved in with him.

During one school holiday, I was sent to visit my father's aunt who had survived the war. She schooled me in how to beg my parents to make up, a scheme that was doomed to failure. During that trip she took me to a farm where I found a kitten which I tortured terribly, until she stopped me. I don't know whether that poor kitten survived. By then, having already suffered occasional depersonalisation episodes, I was clearly a disturbed child, adding animal cruelty to my list of bad deeds.

Eventually, I understood that things had changed. My mother used to visit me at the schoolmarm's, sometimes with my stepfather-to-be. I would ask her to take me home, which made her angry. When I asked why I couldn't go home with her, she would say I had to stay with the schoolmarm because children were not allowed to live in my future stepfather's apartment where she was now living. I didn't believe her. I knew it was because she thought I was very bad.

My space in the schoolmarm's apartment was the green chaise longue in the centre of the lounge room, where I slept. Its coarse fabric rubbed roughly against my face as I cried bitter tears at my abandonment, but no one cared. I learnt to hate school. It started on the first day when I attempted to kiss the teacher because she looked pretty. She was appalled and did not want me to kiss her, although finally, she relented when I insisted, embarrassed at her refusal. Then she told me not to kiss her again. It wasn't done at school. In contrast, I had been my preschool teacher's favourite. She sometimes asked my parents whether I was allowed to go home with her and would take me home for the night as a treat. I could eat as many conserved Morello cherries as I wanted at her place.

The schoolteacher, however, did not like me. She never thought my writing was neat enough to exhibit on the wall like the other children's, although I tried my hardest. She also didn't believe me when I said I needed to go to the toilet. Eventually, I started to wet my pants and was embarrassed when everyone in the class heard the splish-splash of my urine cascade onto the wooden floor. The teacher was not pleased. She reported it to the schoolmarm's husband when he came to pick me up. He was gentle and understanding, but his wife was harsh and showed her disgust each time he reported a new accident to her.

The schoolmarm's adult son and his wife lived in the other half of her very large apartment, and they had a daughter who was a little older than me. The daughter collected serviettes. Each type had to have the same designs but be in different colours. I wanted to collect serviettes too, and ended up with a small collection. Sometimes, we were taken for walks and picked up the wild chestnuts that had fallen off the trees along the Danube. Back upstairs, the granddaughter taught me to make them into tiny chairs, tables, and other objects with the use of pins stuck in the appropriate places. It hurt my fingers to push the pins into the hard surface of the chestnuts, but I enjoyed the game very much.

The granddaughter was obviously favoured over me by the adults, as was her right, although I could not understand this as I thought myself prettier. Her parents were, however, nice to me. I was known for singing popular love songs and they must have heard me because her father promised to organise an audition for me with the Hungarian Opera. After much begging, it was finally arranged, and I remember how the fine lady with the very red lipstick who listened to my singing suddenly broke into a very high and loud note, correcting the pitch that I had apparently not reached to her satisfaction. She advised that I should learn to play the piano and come back when I was older. I never made it back because the revolution broke out soon afterwards.

Sometimes when my mother came to visit, she would take me down to the local café. She said I could have any of the delicious cakes on display, but I saw through the blackmail and broke our unexpressed contract—my injunction not to have any emotional needs—by insisting that I didn't want any cakes, I just wanted her to take me home. She would look very annoyed and tell me that it was not possible. As a peace offering, she once bought me a huge new doll made of hard plastic, not soft like my favourite ragdoll, which she often criticised as being grubby and awful. I didn't want the hard plastic doll and kept repeating that I just wanted her to take me home, although I could tell that this made her very angry.

There were also pleasant Sundays when my mother came to pick me up with my stepfather-to-be. He brought along his son Gabi from his first marriage, and the four of us would go out for the day to Vidampark, an amusement park in Budapest. I liked Gabi, who was two years my senior, and enjoyed those days, except when my balloons invariably popped. My stepfather-to-be prevented my inevitable crying by making tiny balloons with the busted remnants. He would stretch and then suck the balloon pieces until they swelled inside his mouth, and then pull them out and tie them up tightly. On those fun days out, it was even more upsetting to be returned to the schoolmarm's formal apartment.

The Hungarian Revolution started on 23 October 1956. It was a nationwide revolt against Communism, the Marxist–Leninist government of the then-Hungarian People's Republic and its Soviet-imposed policies that had been in place since the end of World War II.

We only just managed to get out alive. This was of course not my mother's first escape from death. Just over a decade earlier, when she was a 19-year-old arriving in Auschwitz, she was separated from her sister and placed in a line destined for the gas chambers, together with other prisoners who were deemed unable to work. Her sister, my aunt, had been allocated to slave labour, but the SS noticed that my mother, who was born with a twisted hip, walked with a limp and they quickly determined her fate. When the SS soldier walked further down the line, my aunt quickly pulled my mother back to the slave labour line, and she survived. Another time she was again ordered to stand in a line. Those in line were told they were going on a holiday. A woman approached my mother in the line and begged her to swap places with her, desperate to get out. My mother thought of her sister, who was very ill at the time with hepatitis in the camp's hospital. She agreed to swap with the woman so she could continue to sneak her own portion of dreadful root soup into the hospital and help her sister regain her strength. It was later revealed that the 'holiday' destination had been the gas chambers.

On the day the revolution started, I stood on tiptoe on the balcony of the schoolmarm's apartment with her granddaughter, trying to catch sight of the crowd of students gathered in front of the parliament building that was decorated with a red star and huge banners of Lenin and Stalin. I am not sure whether I remember this or have heard it, but a male and a female student had been lifted onto a statue of a famous Hungarian poet, when the cheering from the crowd was suddenly mixed with eerie thuds ricocheting against the buildings, then silence. The two students tumbled down like ragdolls.

The schoolmarm's granddaughter and I were quickly ushered inside, away from the balcony. The balcony doors were firmly shut and the radio was turned on, just in time for the announcement of the revolution.

The one good thing about the revolution was that I didn't have to go to school. There were some close calls during this time. I remember the chandelier swinging above me when the bombers dropped their load; the shattered windowpanes; showers of glass shards on the Persian rug. I remember the ominous sound of the sirens and the hasty evacuation of everyone living in the apartment block to the cellar. I remember the discomfort of being forced to go to the toilet in public down there, but there was no other option.

One day while we were down in the cellar, a Russian soldier suddenly pushed the door open, and everyone's eyes were transfixed upon his machinegun. It was a very tense moment. One resident who could speak Russian asked him not to shoot us, as we had not done anything to him. At this, he turned slowly and walked back out the door.

Another time we had no bread left in the apartment, and I was allowed to go with the schoolmarm's maid to the bakers. We joined a long queue. As we stood there waiting, we heard loud rumbling and felt the vibration of approaching tanks. My first response was excitement. A Russian soldier was standing up in the first tank, scouting. He spotted us looking at him and I wanted him to like me. Perhaps I smiled. Next, we noticed the gun on the tank slowly turn in our direction. Without another thought, the maid grabbed my hand and we fled the queue. We ran as fast as we could until we reached the portal of the nearest block of apartments, with the tank following us. We pushed open the heavy wooden door of the portal leading into the courtyard, and once inside we leaned against the door with all our weight until it shut. My forehead rested against the rough wood, my eyes squeezed tightly shut, waiting for the thud, waiting to die.

When does a child learn to expect death? How did I know to expect death? After a while, when nothing happened, I opened my eyes. Then I tentatively helped the maid pull open the heavy door again. We looked right and left and saw that the tank had disappeared.

Then it seemed as if we would have peace. The schoolmarm's entire household gathered around the radio as it was announced that Hungary was 'now neutral'. There was much cheering in the lounge room, but although everyone seemed to believe this, I somehow felt there was something inauthentic about the joyousness, that the adults were willingly allowing themselves to be deluded. My hunch turned out to be true, as the deafening sound of airplanes just above, the bombing, the shooting, and the insistent continuous moan of the warning sirens returned with hardly a pause.

Food was scarce during the revolution, and people often queued for hours outside grocery shops and bakeries. My father was the head of the department that controlled the import and export of fruit and vegetables in Hungary, and he would sometimes dodge bullets and tanks to cross Budapest and reach the schoolmarm's apartment unannounced with a parcel of food for the schoolmarm's family so that I, too, would have sufficient and nutritious food to eat. The scarcity of food was such that one day we were eating soup, and I thought it tasted delicious—until I found out that the meat in the soup was horsemeat. I loved horses and left the soup, swearing that I would never eat horsemeat again.

The revolution seemed to go on for a very long time but in reality, it lasted only about two months. Then, after what seemed to be daily warning sirens, a scramble down to the cellar, and unending sitting and silent waiting until we could go back upstairs, there was suddenly feverish action. I was leaving the schoolmarm's apartment with my father and his girlfriend Lili, and we were on our way to the central Budapest train station. There we met my mother and stepfather-to-be and took a train to Győr, the town where my father and I were born and where my mother grew up. My aunt and her family still lived there, and we went to ask if they wanted to come along. They decided to stay and so we said our goodbyes. It was one of the coldest winters in Hungary and we all wore several layers, mainly because we hadn't taken suitcases so as not to raise suspicions about our intended escape.

Then we were back on the train, which stopped at the last Hungarian station before the Austrian border. Suddenly, there was much shouting, everyone had to get off, and the platform was crawling with police and army personnel. Despite the protests of my parents, we were ushered into a small very crowded holding room along with others who looked as if they had also planned to flee across the border. The guard momentarily left the room to round up more suspects. In that moment, my father motioned to my mother and stepfather and moved to the door. I remember my stepfather questioning this risky action, but soon we were outside, walking as normally as any traveller would, towards the station exit.

Once we reached the village, we had a rendezvous with a waiter at a small inn. There were two waiters, but only one of them, who wore a visual clue, was the right man, and I understood that it was vitally important not to approach the wrong one. My father went in and spoke to the waiter, who gave him an address and a password. Then we were walking again and soon leaving the village, taking the snaking country road bordered by snow-covered fields. Truck after truck sped past us towards Budapest, their open trays laden with those poor individuals who had been funnelled into the holding room at the station. There was tension as they approached. Perhaps a truck would stop to load us on, but again, luck was with us.

Eventually we arrived at the farmhouse and were asked for the password provided by the waiter, and only then were we allowed inside the dimly lit main room with tightly drawn curtains. There, we were to wait for the guide who would lead us across the border during the night. As our eyes adjusted, we saw that the room was crowded with 20 very quiet young men as well as the farmer's children. We settled beside the young men and were told to remain silent.

Hours passed, and with them, our unease about the length of the wait. It was now deep night. Whispered doubts arose as to whether the guide would even turn up. Then, just when it seemed that he would never arrive, he was suddenly at the door and we were all silently following him into the blackness of the night. As we filed out, my parents demanded that I leave behind my ragdoll, which I was clutching, for the gypsy children living at the farmhouse. I objected, but to no avail. Soon, we were walking across snowy fields amongst the prickly remains of the harvest, wading into the odd muddy hole, and slipping on wet vegetation. After a while we stopped for a rest. I was shivering and shaking. I remember my mother asking if I was cold. I said I wasn't, and it was true. I wasn't cold, I was terrified. It was hard to walk and I couldn't keep up, so the young men eventually decided to take turns carrying me on their shoulders.

We had walked for a while when somewhere in the gloom we heard a baby cry, and instantly a flare lit up the sky, searching for escapees. Our guide whispered for us to get down and keep silent. After another flare went up, they stopped looking for us, and the young couple with the baby approached our group, asking if they could join us. The guide agreed and we started walking again. After a long time, we saw a figure in the distance. It was a border guard. Our guide walked over to talk to him. They talked for a while, and then the guide came back to lead us silently over the border.

Then followed lights, noise, voices, taxis waiting to ferry us, and a strange tasting hot chocolate, which I later learnt was made with milk powder, handed to me through the taxi window by Red Cross volunteers. We had arrived in Austria, and we were safe. I, my mother, stepfather, father, and stepmother were amongst the 200,000 people who fled Hungary some time before the revolution ended.

In Austria, we slept on straw on the floor of a large barn-like building together with other refugees. I have a memory of my mother standing outside completely naked and washing her private parts one morning, scooping the water with her hand from a white enamel washbasin, cleaning her vagina harshly, perhaps disgustedly, angrily.

During the day we were free to go outside, and on the first day in Vienna my mother sold one of her gold rings for a pittance to buy me a banana, as I had never tasted one. I disappointed her by not liking it.

My family got out of Hungary just before the Russians finally crushed the revolution. By then, almost all countries offering asylum had closed their doors. There was just one country left, Denmark.

'Where is Denmark?' my mother asked. It was a country that had obviously never previously been a conscious part of her world. On 29 November 1956, we boarded a train with the remainder of the fleeing Hungarians, travelling north across Austria and Germany. At one German station, the platform was crowded with Germans donating all sorts of goods to us refugees through the train's windows. A brown rubber boy doll was thrust at me. I knew that we did not like Germans for some reason, but here were these people with a full heart, wishing us well. It was evening by the time the train pulled in at Padborg Station in Denmark, bringing with it the last of the 1,000 Hungarians who were destined to call Denmark home.

For me, Denmark instantly became synonymous with safety and freedom. There were no tanks, no sirens warning us to seek shelter, no deafening bombings, no shards of glass raining down on me, no mortal threat. Also, unlike in Hungary, where bribery was often the only way to obtain what you needed, Danes trusted their citizens to be honest, to abide by the law, and to demand their human rights. Refugees discussed with incredulity how they had watched the milkman leave milk bottles at the front doors of houses, and that no one had stolen them. This was a completely different culture from the one we had left behind.

The Danish sky was December grey and a fresh and unforgiving wind blew relentlessly. A strong smell of seaweed greeted us at the children's summer camp, where we had to stay until the authorities found us permanent accommodation. I quickly learnt, after I accidentally broke a finger in a door while running around exploring the new environment with the other refugee children, that Danish design and building standards in general were much more exacting than in Hungary. We children also discovered mint-flavoured toothpaste in the bathrooms, a novelty unavailable in post-war Hungary. We must have eaten many grams of the stuff before it came to the notice of the distracted adults.

My father and Lili were taken to a different refugee camp, and as my mother and stepfather were otherwise engaged, trying to make arrangements for the immediate future, I was largely left to my own devices for the first time in my life. On weekdays, the refugee children were bussed to the local school. On the first day at recess, I found myself alone in the middle of the playground. With my dark curls and thick sheepskin coat, an abundance of blond children were eyeing me off and slowly moving towards me. I turned to see curious children closing in on me from all directions. In an instant I ripped off the thick leather belt around my waist and swung it around my body. The invaders stopped dead. Some made frightened sounds and those closest to me moved away in self-defence. At that moment I learnt that being tough and aggressive gave me power and kept me safe.

After school, the beach just beyond the summer camp buildings became my playground. Cold green waves rolled to the shore with a sound and rhythm I had never experienced before. Although I had been to Lake Balaton, there was no ocean or smelly seaweed in Hungary, nor an abundance of sand, or small rubbish dumps like the one on this beach. Sometimes when the rubbish was waiting to be burnt, I would walk amongst it to look for empty tins. Then I would mix and stir sand and seawater together with a stick until I was satisfied that the bubbling substance resembled the exact colour of milky coffee. The next day, I would repeat it all.

So finally, at the age of seven, I could play completely alone outside in the weather to my heart's content with sand, water, and treasures I found amongst the rubbish. And I was back with my mother.

CHAPTER 16

I've been sitting by Viggo's bed on the rigid tan armchair for hours.

'It's almost dinnertime,' I tell him.

'Oh, no! I don't want any dinner.'

He wrinkles his face in disgust. A nurse comes in to give him his medication. He has become more and more selective about what he will eat. Initially, I rushed home at night to cook him meals that he normally enjoys, but the other day he refused my home-cooked dinner and told me to stop bringing him anything. He would just eat whatever hospital food was provided.

I always check his breakfast tray if it hasn't yet been collected in the mornings when I arrive at the palliative care unit. Lately, I have noticed that he has hardly touched any of the food.

The doctors have ordered an end to the intravenous drips and the removal of all his lines 'for the time being'. Viggo is relieved. He can now move without getting tangled up, but as he no longer gets any saline solution, I worry that he doesn't drink enough. It's too much hard work for him, especially now that he can only drink thickened water. Normal water makes him cough and panic.

'You know what will happen if you don't eat and drink!' I warn him, suddenly frightened.

'Yes, I know,' he says wearily.

I know that people lose their appetite towards the end of their life. But I can't help admonishing him; it's the Yiddishe mama in me. It's so hard to watch him missing meals.

I go outside to the communal kitchen so he can't see me or smell the food that I eat, guilty because he has gone without. Should I encourage him to eat? I decide that I will offer him a drink or something to eat from time to time and refrain from making comments if he refuses.

The food trolley arrives and he accepts his thickened water before waving the attendants away. I later add the thickened water to the other half a dozen already in the little bar fridge next to the bathroom door. As we silently sit, waiting for another night to fall, my thoughts return to the past.

Once Upon a Love

*

After the trip to Denmark in 1975, I walked around with an enormous pain in my heart. It felt big and heavy and sad and melancholy. I daydreamt about Viggo, wondering whether he would ever come to Australia. He was constantly on my mind. I was burning for him. One day at teachers' college, I was walking down the stairs after a tutorial and I looked up to the opposite wall and thought I saw Viggo's face projected there. I was almost living in another world where Viggo was ever-present in some strange way.

I tried going out with other men because I thought we could never be, and because I rarely heard from him, but that only made it worse. Every man I dated reinforced for me how impossible it was to recapture the feelings I had for Viggo. I simply needed to be with him. My pain led me to drink and smoke and study and have one-night stands. I became quite wild again. All the time, I wondered whether there would be a letter from him that day, or if not, perhaps the next day. My heart limped from one day to the next. Each day started with hope, and then when no letter came, I was awash with disappointment and despair. At the end of each day, the cycle started again, and I'd cling to the hope that perhaps his letter would arrive the next day. That was how it was for months. I don't remember exactly how long it went on.

In the meantime back in Denmark after his separation, Viggo was living in a house that was too large for him, in a suburb filled with families. Life seemed drab and mundane, empty and purposeless, working and then coming home to an empty house.

This continued month after month until 1976 when one of his sisters suggested they take a trip to Israel together. He had always wanted to see Israel, and wrote to me enthusiastically about it. Emboldened, I wrote back and pointed out that if he could travel there, then he could just as easily come to Australia. Viggo thought about this for a while and the following Easter, made up his mind. He told his boss to expect him back in three weeks. His boss was surprised at this sudden turn of events from an otherwise predictable and punctual architect.

Viggo packed, certain now that he had to see me again in order to work out his own life. He needed to know whether we could be together or not. It was a big trip for him. In his hurry, he left without a visa and was stopped in Bucharest, where he spent three very cold days in his summer clothes, appropriate for the Australian climate. He turned up daily at the Australian Embassy to ask whether they had granted him a visa overnight, while I was pulling strings at my end, calling Canberra. Finally, he was allowed onto a plane to Sydney.

I was waiting for him, searching for his face amongst the emerging passengers, hardly believing that he had really made the plane, concerned that they had perhaps not allowed him to fly out after all.

He later told me how he had spotted me. 'You were standing there in your blue denim culottes and a very colourful blouse. You were so thin; you were always thin at that time. You were so vulnerable, your body was so ... worn out, but your arms were strong, muscular.'

Yes, of course I was thin. I had been pining for him for so long! And as for my arms, carrying little ones for years had made them strong.

Our reunion was immensely joyful, lighthearted, intense, and passionate. We could not believe we were together at last, we could not get enough of each other, we were unable to walk next to each other without touching or kissing or entirely melting into a tight embrace. At night we slept in each other's arms in my single bed.

Then I arranged for the children to stay with Michael and we took a trip up north, visiting the sights. On the way, we found a secluded waterfall where the water splashed into a deep and inviting pool. We took off our clothes and swam in the icy water. We had no money and slept in the car. One evening, we parked at a lake where there were some camping facilities. The sound of sniggering and laughing from other campers woke us up the next morning. I sat up and looked out at a pelican sailing by the front window of the car, and realised that we had parked at low tide and the car was now well and truly in the water. Fortunately, we were able to back it out without getting stuck. Sometimes when Viggo drove, I serenaded him on the guitar which I had taken along on the trip.

Our hearts were breaking at the thought of our imminent parting, but after three weeks in Australia, Viggo returned to Denmark. However, he was only returning to pack up. He came back on a visa as my fiancé nominee in September 1977 and he brought Denmark with him. I was no longer homesick. He embodied the safety and freedom I had found there as a child.

When Viggo moved in, only the bare necessities of life such as work, study, being with the children, shopping, cooking, and eating could prevent us from physically melting together. There was a constant palpable sexual tension between us, a thirst to fully merge into each other somehow, and we sensed a continual frustration at the barrier of our physical bodies. Our desire for each other was unquenchable. Viggo described it as wanting to become one with me. One memorable day we were passing each other in the wide corridor that also housed a piano and we started to kiss. Next, we were making passionate love on the piano keyboard lid. On weekend trips away when the children were with their father, we would sometimes pull over to the side of the road to continue where we had left off some hours before, and then drive on again. I was mostly the instigator, hungering for his body. Once, after making love yet again, Viggo warned me that I should not expect this level of lovemaking to continue. At the time I thought it was a strange statement. He must have become quite frightened by my sexual hunger, and anxious about his adequacy to quell it. For him, our love was not necessarily connected to lovemaking, whereas for me it was its culmination.

During this first sweet period, our joy in each other was borrowed from the mundane reality of life with two children who lived with us when they were not with their father. I remembered my stepfather's brutal take on his parenting role and announced to Viggo that the children came first for me, and that they already had a father and did not need another. I need not have worried. He was only interested in having a relationship with me. The children seemed like an annoying intrusion into his very private world; too loud, too personal, too disruptive, and too messy. I laughed it off, but it was reminiscent of the ice-cream incident on the beach in Denmark, a continuation of his distinct separateness from us.

Throughout all the years we had known each other, we had not really known each other at all. Perhaps you can only really know a person when you live with them. Now, our enormous differences were being revealed. I was creative and messy, while Viggo needed order and was obsessively clean. He was quiet, private, and withdrawn and I was outgoing, loud, friendly, welcoming, and novelty-seeking. His idea of socialising was to plan and stick to a firm date, while I offered an open house with wine and coffee to whoever wanted to drop by.

Almost immediately, we clashed about who should be responsible for contraception, and while this was unresolved, I become pregnant. Viggo was adamant that I should have an abortion. He had only recently started work for a Danish architect who had schooled him in the local requirements but could not pay him much, and he wasn't ready to have a child. Although I pleaded with him, I also had to face my own conscience, as I had been drinking excessively, unaware that I was pregnant. My initial use of alcohol to quell the pain of missing Viggo had become an ingrained habit and continued after he moved in. I also thought about the fact that I had almost completed my studies in early childhood. If I had a child now, I would not be able to work in the field for years, and without work experience I might never get a job in my chosen profession. So with a heavy heart I agreed to abort our baby, our first child made from our tender, deep love. I was devastated and cried, heartbroken, for entire days following the abortion.

We also had to deal with the pressure of having to get married, as Viggo had arrived on a fiancé visa, but we could not agree on the venue. I suggested an outdoor wedding at Lane Cove National Park, and although Viggo didn't have an alternative suggestion, he was adamant we not marry there. It was too public a place where everyone turned up with their eskies and their kids.

The venue wasn't really the problem. It was more the fact that we had each had one marriage failure. This time, we both needed to be sure and while we now shared a house, our relationship was far from committed. Viggo kept himself very separate. He secreted away in a safe place the fine designer objects he had brought from Denmark. Groceries and other expenses were shared unequally between us, as the children were mine. I told the children that he was not their father, and not to call him 'Dad', fearing a repeat of my own bad experience with stepfathers. The children were high maintenance and Viggo frequently found their intense energy and noise overwhelming.

Other issues arose, creating conflict between us. I had been used to being the homemaker and making my own decisions, with Michael largely absent. I also felt it was my role as a mother. One day, I brought home a monstrous knitted object made by one of the adult disabled students I was working with at the time.

I thought it was very arty and hung it in a corner of the lounge room. Viggo objected strongly, and over the next few weeks he kept up the objections relentlessly until the 'artwork' ended up in the garage, as did other things he disliked. Because he was an architect, he was convinced that of the two of us, he was better qualified to make such decisions. Later, in the house he eventually designed for us in Westleigh, I arranged the furniture downstairs in the lounge room when we moved in, only to find the arrangement changed when I next entered the room. I gritted my teeth and changed it all back, and later Viggo changed it again. He even designed the bedroom so the bed could only fit against a particular part of one wall, and we lived for years without a proper clothesline, because he thought a clothesline would spoil the look of the place. We never talked about it; it was a silent war, a war of wills, and eventually I gave up.

Viggo was intensely private and rarely shared about himself. He was often dismissive towards the children's and my effusiveness. When visitors came, he would sit somewhere away in a corner and not contribute to the conversation. I finally abandoned my many attempts at including him, increasingly irritated at his heavy energy that dragged down the merriment in the room.

I wasn't sure that the relationship would last and so rather than make concessions for his having newly arrived, I often went out and left him on his own. As time went by, it seemed that we just existed alongside each other in the house. I made sure I always had one foot out the door, flirting with other men. I wrote songs that often involved faux relationships that mainly existed in my fantasy, and played them on my guitar. Nevertheless, our mutual physical attraction never waned.

As time passed, Viggo took more interest in the children and they warmed to his calm presence. We took them on holidays, picnics, weekend excursions. One weekend when the children were with their father, Viggo and I went away to the country. On the way to our destination, I spotted a sign for baby goats by the side of the road. I dragged a reluctant Viggo in to have a look and we walked out with a baby goat, which was added to the family cats and the budgerigar. The children loved the goat and all his antics. One time when he was off his leash, he ran inside the house and jumped onto the children's bunk bed. Another time he escaped and ate the neighbour's roses. By then, Viggo had been granted permanent residency, and we packed the children, the goat, the cats, and the bird into the car, dropped them off with Michael, and flew back to Denmark to visit friends and family. Being by ourselves made it an adult trip and reinvigorated our feelings for each other. We were in love again and ready to have a baby.

I became pregnant with Josh soon after our trip, three years after Viggo moved to Australia. It happened during a particularly tender lovemaking moment and we were both aware of it. Viggo cried afterwards. When I asked him why he had cried, he said it was because he was passing his life on to the next generation. He seemed to perceive having sowed his genes as a first step towards his own demise.

The letter that Viggo wrote to me when he was on a business trip demonstrates his thoughts about our relationship during that time:

Dear Mimi, Thank you for your letter which I received yesterday. I think our trip to Denmark got me to really feel that we belong together—I felt like living again, not waiting any longer for tomorrow. I realised that it was important to live in the here and now and say 'yes' to us and a common future one way or another with a child of our own. I also feel strongly attached to both Rebecca and Cassandra and feel the development of their acceptance and their joy in us all being together. We have somehow overcome the first difficulties and have slipped into a lovely warm relationship with each other. You and I, the children and I hope Junior [later known as Joshua] *will also find his place amongst us all. I love you xxxxxxxxxxxx*

By then, I had been working as an early childhood teacher and maternity leave had to be taken when I was seven months pregnant. I used the last two months to write my first books about early childhood activities. Although the baby brought us all closer as a family, Viggo and I continued to clash over our differences. He was often annoyed at my children's noisiness and frequently in a bad mood. His withdrawn behaviour forced me to mentally defend myself. I did this by ignoring him, being scathing and angry, especially when I had invited friends over and he would be in a corner, resting his elbows on his knees or on a table, his chin in his palms, oozing judgement and negativity in our direction. He was clearly trying to freeze my friends out. In my embarrassment over his behaviour and to show him that I wasn't affected, I responded by becoming even more cheerful and loud.

Several of my friends became involved in new self-discovery type personal development courses. The courses involved meditation and I was averse to anything interfering with my consciousness. I had tried yoga a few times and disliked the feeling of coming to after a guided meditation without knowing what happened to me during it. Yoga and eastern religions were clearly not for me.

Religion in general was anathema, as I had changed from believing in God to being an atheist—until a very strange incident just before Viggo moved in with me. I was sleeping with four-year old Rebecca one night. We were lying facing each other and in my dream, I suddenly saw a channel open from my forehead to hers, and had an instant three-fold understanding that she was at the same time me, herself, ancient, and much more knowledgeable than I. The whole thing was so real that I immediately woke up. I could not forget the experience and the next day I went to the library to try to find out whether there was anything to know about a channel emanating from the forehead. My research first led me to the chakras, then to Carl Jung's autobiography and other writings.

My search for truth and a purpose had begun. From then on, I paid more attention to my dreams if they seemed to be telling me about the future or to what I called 'messages' that I received in a variety of ways. I eventually also signed up for the personal development courses. They were designed to free people from their old unhelpful belief systems and long-buried pain. During the second course, I realised that I had become an alcoholic. My stepfather had occasionally made scathing statements about me during my childhood, for example that I was like my father and that I would become an alcoholic just like him. So I was deeply shocked at my own discovery. I plunged into a deep depression and intense self-hate for a while and then gave up alcohol cold turkey.

The courses also improved my relationship with my mother and stepfather, and I found myself forgiving them for their injustices to me during my childhood.

I changed and grew rapidly both spiritually and psychologically as a result of the courses, and I knew that Viggo would have to grow with me if our relationship was to survive. He seemed so set in his ways and determined to stay that way. One time when we were in the city, I broke into a happy, carefree skip down George Street and laughingly tried to drag him with me. Instead, he yanked his arm back, annoyed at my 'immaturity'. He was so heavy and stuck. I needed him to lighten up, to be more spontaneous and lighthearted. I wanted to bring him out of his defensive, stiffly adult space. Although Viggo had told me when he arrived in Australia that in Copenhagen, he had been interested in learning meditation, was interested in eastern philosophy, reflexology, reading works such as *The Prophet*, and keen to find out more, he didn't seem to want to change and refused to be budged. Then, one day when I had given up ever convincing him and thought our relationship was doomed, he announced that he had signed up for a course.

He had been right to worry about signing up, because it turned out there were many skeletons inside his defensive withdrawn quietness. The courses were confronting, taking people back to fearful places where traumas unravelled, and they took Viggo back to his family of origin. His family had been poor and working class, living in a tiny inner-city apartment where he and his two older sisters shared one bedroom. Viggo now recalled times when his mother, Viola, would try to prevent his drunken father from entering the bedroom on evenings after a long day at work. One such night Viggo heard a drunken commotion outside the bedroom. His mother was shouting, and then his father entered and lay down with his sister in her bed, which was next to Viggo's. He heard his mother cry in the other room, and then she barged in. She pulled Viggo out of his bed, saying that he shouldn't be there, whisking him into the fine lounge room that was only ever used on Sundays or when they had visitors. She told him to stay there with her for the duration of whatever was taking place.

These frequent incidents of sexual abuse may have been the trigger that unleashed Viola's bipolar illness. Her own mother had died soon after her birth, and a few years later her sailor father's ship went down, leaving her an orphan. An aunt had taken her in, but it was a tough childhood marked by hard physical work and very little affection. During Viola's occasional hospitalisations for bipolar disorder, Viggo and his sisters would either stay with friends of the family, or in orphanages. One especially traumatic time when

Viggo was separated from his sisters, he was dressed in the orphanage's 'pooh- coloured uniform', a colour he hated from that time onwards. He never knew when or if his parents would be back to take him home, mirroring my own experience during my time with the schoolmarm. He was always told to be quiet and undemanding, even before his mother was hospitalised. So when I met him, he was a gentle, shy, quiet guy, earnestly yearning for love and attachment—and for a very strong woman, unlike his mother. We were both desperate for love and equally terrified of abandonment, unaware that these emotions would both fuel and plague our relationship.

His first personal development course spanned a couple of weekday nights, and he seemed to enjoy them. This was followed by an intensive weekend. The Saturday night program included a meditation, and he had a stirring vision. He saw me come downstairs towards him, wearing a white wedding dress. The vision was a revelation, clarifying for him that we should marry. He could hardly wait to tell me that he wanted to get married now, that it was all he had ever really wanted. But it was late by the time he came home, and I had gone to bed, leaving him a note on the kitchen table.

The same night that Viggo was at the course, I had been unable to sleep, going over the many times I had been disdainful towards him. I thought how badly I had treated him, not even caring whether we stayed together, whereas he had given up his whole life to be with me. So I panicked, terrified of losing him. What if he realised I was no good for him, or he met someone else on the course? Such courses brought out intense feelings and created instant connections between participants. At the thought of losing him, I was once again flooded with enormous love and felt ready for a deep, committed, intimate relationship. I was ready to marry him, and that was what I wrote in the note I left for him on the kitchen table. Then I fell asleep.

When Viggo got home, he could hardly believe his eyes as he read my note and he just had to wake me up. Again, we had arrived at the same place at exactly the same time, just as when we had thought about each other before we met up again after eight years apart, and just like when our letters had crossed the world at the same time after I returned to Australia. At some very deep level, we could tap into a place where we were in permanent connection, in a quantum-type entanglement, in total harmony, regardless of our outward daily conflicts. We were feeling and thinking similarly and simultaneously, regardless of distance and time. It was so strange.

The courses we took helped us confront and resolve at least some of our traumatic experiences, and so we felt free to love more truly. We got married on 1 September 1984, seven years after Viggo joined me in

Australia, surrounded by friends, family, and a house full of wildly grown freesias that we had hand-picked with the children. I learnt later that freesias symbolise friendship, trust, and innocence, and appropriately, we felt entirely devoted, virginal, and innocently open to each other.

CHAPTER 17

I had gone back to full-time work in 1982 when Joshua was 11 months, as Viggo was anxious about not being able to support us all. So much so, that when eight-year-old Rebecca wanted to take piano lessons, Viggo refused to pay for them and said she had to wait until I returned to work.

Viggo's anxiety about money dated back to his father's sudden death when Viggo was nine. Well-meaning adults had told him that from then on, he would be the man of the house and had to look after the family. He had taken this to heart, even though he was the baby of the family. He clearly could not look after a family at the time, but he had never recovered from his feelings of helplessness and inadequacy since. He continually feared that he would not be able to *slå til*, a Danish expression meaning to be good enough, to live up to expectations. The feeling had followed him into adulthood, and he feared that he would not be able to properly support his family.

This was one area where we were perfectly matched. Viggo was, on the one hand, strongly motivated to protect and look after me—the Hungarian refugee—but on the other, he felt powerless to do so. Initially, this fitted well with my father's injunctions that I must not be weak and naïve like other women, a philosophy I had internalised. I was independent and strong, a born 'women's libber', just the woman Viggo needed.

Additionally, I had witnessed my mother's weakness and memorised this as lessons in what to avoid. I clearly remembered the day we had gone for a walk, she pushing my new little brother in a pram, and I, around 10 years old. During the walk, I atypically took the opportunity of having my mother to myself and asked her to protect me from my stepfather's beatings.

It was always the same. His blows would come from nowhere, without warning, and knock the wind out of me. I would panic because I couldn't breathe. Then, my mother confessed how my stepfather had raped her on their wedding night. I didn't know what rape was, but it sounded violent, and I wanted to protect her immediately. I said she should leave him, that I would support her and help her cope, but she felt she couldn't, and that was the end of the conversation. Nothing changed, and for years afterwards, my mother allowed my stepfather to bully us, emotionally abuse me, and brutally bash us children.

He had started on me soon after my mother and he were married. He'd decided to teach me to read Hungarian, resulting in many hours of gruelling verbal abuse. This was followed by maths tuition, when he would call me names and hit me for not trying harder. One particularly awful event stands out. I was about nine years old and had been out playing with a friend. I arrived home five minutes later than the time I was supposed to be back. As I put the key in the lock, my stepfather tore the door open and felled me with all his might.

He also brought in reinforcements. Soon after we had settled in Denmark, he arranged for his mother to come out from Hungary to join us, so for a while, before my brother was born, it felt very much like there were two camps: my stepfather and his mother against my mother and me. The old woman was careful not to incite my stepfather's ire by criticising my mother, but she made sure she reported every one of my misdeeds—even suspected ones—each night at the dinner table, as proof of my inborn wickedness and further evidence of her own family's superiority. During one dinner while my mother was pregnant, the old woman motioned towards me and entertained us with the theory that children could get very jealous and kill their small siblings. I was surprised, pleased, and felt secretly vindicated when my mother defended me and said I would never do such a thing.

Nevertheless, the old woman's presence was tolerated for years. It was only after I found my disorientated stepfather on the floor of the master bedroom one day, surrounded by empty pill bottles, that our home life changed for the better. Shocked at the sight, I immediately alerted my mother, who asked me to run down to the phone booth and call the ambulance. After my stepfather was taken away, the old woman wondered aloud why he would have done such a thing, finally suggesting that he must have been driven to it by me during the maths coaching the night before. My mother's reaction was instant. She smashed her fist through the reinforced glass coffee tabletop and yelled at her to get out. The old woman was offended and asked me to go down and call a taxi. She didn't need to ask me twice. I ran all the way to the phone booth. When I returned, my mother looked stressed, wondering how my stepfather would react, whispering that I shouldn't have gone. But the deed was done, and the old lady moved to Pista's parents' place and stayed there for what seemed like a long time.

Despite all this, my mother never attempted to free herself from my stepfather, never learnt to drive, allowing even her mobility to be entirely dependent upon him. I, having witnessed all this, was determined never to give a man such power over me.

With the personal development coursework I had undertaken, I had faced and overcome alcohol addiction and was now on a quest to heal my spirit. I had arrived at a point where I longed to cast off my strong woman persona and allow myself to be sensitive and feminine, to stay at home and look after the family. I longed to surrender, to let down my guard and embody my femininity; to be 'Mother' supported by 'Father'. I wanted Viggo to protect me and provide for us. I wanted to be the woman my father had told me not to be; vulnerable, feminine, trusting. And I longed to have another child, a little sister for Josh.

Leaving Joshua and going back to work had been hard on us both, and he had become very difficult. He was now four years old, a preschooler, and I wanted to spend more time with him. Besides, I was exhausted, burnt out from having studied, worked, been through a marriage break-up and single parenting, started a new relationship, authored books, confronted my alcoholism, and taught dozens of little children for years.

By that time, we had moved into the beautiful new house designed by Viggo. He had bought a piece of land without consulting me and as it was his money, I didn't question him. It was up to him to invest his money as he saw fit, and he had taken out a loan to have it built. The property was a long way from public transport and from the children's school. But after years of making do and renting I felt we deserved to live well and wanted Viggo to take care of us. I felt ready for this. Living in a new home in a new subdivision felt very much as if we had moved up in the world.

Apart from the kitchen, Viggo afforded me little input. I chose red for the cupboards. The block of land was very steep, so he had designed a pole house. I insisted that we needed a clothesline, so he put it under the house where it was steep and rocky and did not take away from the design. We had a major disagreement about the tiles in the bathroom. He insisted that he knew better about interior decoration, and won the argument.

When we walked around in the house, and ran down the stairs, the house moved a little and felt unsafe. When the washing machine was on spin, the whole house rocked. I asked whether the house was safe so Viggo got an engineer out, who confirmed that the house was safe, even if it moved, as it was just the nature of a pole house. Nevertheless, the engineer recommended some steel bracing to make it feel more comfortable, although this only partly addressed the movement of the house. All these issues raised disagreements and ill feelings between us.

In the meantime, a home and garden journal had heard of Viggo's beautiful design and a journalist came knocking on the door one day while he was at work. She asked whether she could write an article about the house and started to interview me. When I told her about how it moved with the washing machine and made me feel unsafe, she immediately decided not to write the article. Viggo had never sought fame and always preferred teamwork to working on his own. However, I have had to live with the guilt of being instrumental in taking away the opportunity of having his design published in an article that might have led to him becoming a well-known architect.

Viggo now had a new job that came with a Volvo company car. A Diner's card was also part of his salary package. It became a family tradition to take the children out to dinner every Friday night. We both wanted our new home to be a place where we could proudly invite our friends, and so we started a tradition of having an open house and brunch on Sundays. We would all walk to the French patisserie on Sunday mornings to pick up delicious pastries, ready for the guests.

Despite our improved circumstances, Viggo was not convinced that we needed another child or that he could support a growing family. He pointed out that we already had three children. Also, contraception continued to be an issue between us. I had taken responsibility for it since the abortion, but now my body needed a break and Viggo refused to use contraception. I thought it unfair that I had to subject my body to various devices, and suggested he have a vasectomy if he did not want more children. He saw a specialist but after some consideration, decided against it. In the meantime, he agreed that I could stop working full time and take on part-time work so that I had more time at home with the children. The contraception issue remained unresolved. I warned Viggo that I would never have another abortion, and that if I had another child, I would not go back to work until the child was older. We were both aware that this stand-off could only lead to one conclusion, and it was not long before I became pregnant.

Although we still had occasional disagreements and problems, I remained madly in love with Viggo. I was so grateful for the opportunity of experiencing a genuine loving relationship, and it was as if our courage to choose love had brought with it all that was good in life. We had a new house, we were married, we had a gorgeous little boy, and now we were expecting a second baby. It was a new life. I felt that I had been given a second chance to be a good wife and mother. A niggling part of me wanted to obliterate the past, wishing that Michael had never happened.

The baby was due late April. I was curious about the date she would be born. One morning, I woke up from a dream where I was lying on the schoolmarm's old chaise lounge from my childhood. I was in labour. Standing around the back of the chaise longue were shadowy figures, my ancestors. We were all waiting for the midwife. Then the door opened, and a bride in a white wedding dress came through the door. I realised the bride was me, but I somehow looked too old to be a bride wearing white. I pondered what the dream might mean.

A few weeks passed and Nicola was two weeks overdue. I was to be induced the following Monday. I was just looking up Monday's date when I heard a flock of kookaburras outside work up to uproarious laughter, and realised that Monday was Michael's and my wedding anniversary. I joined in with the kookaburras, laughing so hard at this twisted cosmic joke that the mucus plug was expelled. But there was still no baby. I went shopping during the weekend and my waters broke in the supermarket. Still no baby, so the following Monday, I was induced and as my dream had tried to tell me, Nicola was born on Michael's and my 18th wedding anniversary, making it impossible to ever forget that I had married him.

My mother and stepfather came to see the baby at the hospital and my mother brought a present for her. When I unwrapped the present and saw that it was a little ragdoll, I burst out crying. I had shed my armour and allowed my vulnerability and femininity to surface, and now it was as if my ragdoll had been returned to me as a reward 30 years after I'd been forced to give it away. I'm not sure whether my mother realised the significance of her present but I was very grateful for this gift from the universe. It was as if my life had come full circle.

Nicola had a 'small chin', a condition that made it difficult for her to feed. She failed to gain weight and I was very concerned about her. To help make her feeding easier, I tried to express, rather unsuccessfully, so I could feed her the breast milk from a bottle. I became sick several times with mastitis and a high fever, and found it almost impossible to look after the home. During that time, Viggo became increasingly withdrawn. He had to work, and he wanted his strong wife back. I, in turn, became more demanding. I wanted to continue buying the designer clothes he always admired on me and things for the children, as I had done when I was working. I especially wanted a dishwasher, as we were now a large family, although my eldest daughter Cassandra was only with us sometimes, as she had moved to her father's place.

I gave up breastfeeding Nicola and once she was bottle fed, she started putting on weight and developing normally. This allowed me some spare time to focus on my spiritual development. Sometime the year before, I had attended a reincarnation workshop where past lives were explored through meditation and bodywork. During the course, I experienced some vague impressions, but wasn't convinced. They had played a particular tune several times, and when I got into my car on the Sunday night at the end of the workshop, the same tune was playing on the radio as soon as I started the motor. That impressed me, and I was intrigued but not convinced. The subject of reincarnation came back to me when, disturbed at Viggo's withdrawal, I had a dream about lying in a sarcophagus as a pharaoh, killed by my wife, who wanted my sacred ring. I interpreted this to mean that Viggo had perhaps been my wife in a past life, wanting my vitality.

I did not feel comfortable living in the house, although it was very beautiful. I still felt unsafe, as the house continued to wobble even after the steel bracing was added. Then one day when I looked out of the bedroom window, I thought I saw what seemed like large faces projected onto the rocks outside the house. The faces were not aboriginal but some other ancient people that I had never seen before. I checked from time to time to see if they reappeared, and sometimes they did. I wondered whether they had lived here a long time before. Perhaps we had built the house on sacred land; perhaps we should not be there at all. It added to my discomfort about living in the house.

A few weeks later, I walked down the stairs to the lounge room and spotted some red dots on the white wall. I went to investigate. The spots looked gum-like, but when I touched them, they were liquid, although they did not run. I showed them to Viggo and he thought that the sap might have bled through from the timber behind the plasterboard. But the area of the spots was much wider than a stud, and they grew day by day, sometimes quite gummy and at other times completely liquid, until the pattern resembled a large butterfly. Eventually, we cleaned the wall and the spots did not return.

Viggo worked until late every night, just managing to get home in time for dinner, so he didn't have much time to spend with our children and he felt very resentful about this. He worried that we would not be able to afford our lifestyle and repay the mortgage unless I went back to work, so each night after dinner he would sit at his drawing table, designing for the extra private jobs he had secured. I refused to leave Nicola, and he became angrier. I tried to reason with him, explaining my needs, but he was fixated on the mortgage. I said I didn't care where we lived, as long as I could be at home with the children—although I don't know whether I really meant it. I liked the idea of our new middle-class existence. We argued more and more frequently. I was earning a bit of extra money by doing remedial reading with local children at home, but this was not enough to help Viggo feel more secure. He wanted me to go back to full-time work.

So the pieces in the jigsaw that had previously fitted so well—his need for a strong woman and my fierce independence—no longer matched. As Irvin Yalom wrote in *Love's Executioner and Other Tales of Psychotherapy*, when one party 'changes and the spouse stays locked in the same position, then the dynamic equilibrium of the marriage often disintegrates', and one of the pair has to either 'forego growth or grow and jeopardise the union' (p. 166). I had grown, and Viggo's old terror of being an inadequate provider won out.

He often withdrew into himself when any issue arose, becoming a polite, quiet, almost mute stranger. He seemed very comfortable inside his withdrawal. In turn, I felt abandoned and hurt at his lack of interest in our gorgeous baby girl. By and by, his withdrawal grew into rage. Ignoring the shaky ground beneath our relationship, he demanded that I go back to work. I refused. We had a small baby, a four-year-old, and two older children. When I'd returned to work after Josh, I had been so torn, having to wrench myself away from his clinging arms and desperate screams, leaving him to teach other preschoolers instead. But I had acquiesced, done as Viggo had asked, against my maternal instincts, and I was not going to do that again.

By then, I had been meditating for years and sometimes during meditation I would see an image or hear some words. One day I heard, 'Kismet is true.' I wondered what that meant. I had heard of Kismet before but didn't know the true meaning of the word, so I went to the library and learnt that it meant 'fate'. As I had always been fiercely independent, I questioned this meditative message, yet felt that it was somehow ominous.

Viggo became increasingly stiff and curt and I sensed hot explosive rage in him that sometimes surfaced when we argued, and he would shout that I should go back to work. His presence became toxic, and the atmosphere between us was loaded with tension. Everything I did annoyed him, like when we were late for his train. I had to drive him to the station in the mornings, but the time it took to feed Nicola due to her feeding problem made it difficult to get organised, and he blamed me whenever we were late and he missed the train.

One day he confessed that he had looked at the kitchen knives while thinking bad thoughts about me. This was the man whose love I had fought fiercely against before finally surrendering. Ours was the love that had melted my tough persona, giving way to trust, to the inner femininity and innate dependency of a mother with small children that I had previously suppressed. After much caution I had finally married him, but this angry behaviour and the thoughts he had confessed were the antithesis of our promise of commitment, intimacy, and eternal devotion. I was grateful for his honesty, but realised that the children and I had to leave, and leave quickly.

I confided my thoughts, and eventually my plans as they firmed up, to my friend Vera, whom I had met at the children's school. She reacted very strangely, pointing out how wonderful Viggo was, how handsome, what a great architect he was, what a lovely life he had created for the family. Alarm bells rang. A friend was supposed to be empathetic. Didn't she understand that my life might be in danger? After all, Viggo had been admitted with bipolar disorder in the past, thinking he was Jesus, for God's sake!

In a flash, I remembered an occasion when Vera had called and asked whether Viggo could go to her house and help her with something. He had never liked her, had found her to be invasive and voyeur-like, so he'd grumbled at being asked but drove over to her place anyway, because she was my friend. When he returned home, he told me that she had met him at the door in a see-through negligée, acting very flirtatious. I dismissed it at the time, trusting Viggo to be faithful, and never brought it up with Vera, thinking nothing of it. But now this incident suddenly came back to me.

Vera had her own business, drove a red sports car, wore stiletto heels, and her daughter attended the same school as mine. There, she had met Michael and had an affair with him immediately after our divorce. When their relationship came to an end, she began to pursue my friendship, almost as if she was more interested in me than in Michael. She told me that when they were together all he had done was talk about me and she became intrigued. I didn't really like her, but she kept on dropping by until I accepted her friendship. Over time we became friendlier, and once I stupidly confided in her what an excellent lover Viggo was. Now I realised that she was probably hankering after him, too.

Vera wanted to know the exact date and time I was leaving. I suspected that she saw my plan to leave as her opportunity. I told her when I planned to leave but no longer trusted her with the details of where I would stay, making out that I hadn't yet decided on the details. I had already experienced one bad divorce, shared custody of Cassandra and Rebecca was a nightmare, and now my plans included obtaining sole custody of mine and Viggo's children. After some enquiries I found out that if the children resided with one parent for a six-week period, it established a precedent, and the court would look favourably upon granting main carer status to that parent. I laid plans to escape and disappear for six weeks. My best friend Edith, who had travelled from the country to visit us over Christmas specifically to assist me, helped with the arrangements.

The day arrived. Viggo left for work as usual, having no idea what was to come. We quickly packed the car and I left with the children, taking only the bare essentials. Nicola was in her car seat, her cot tied onto the roof rack. Before I left, I wrote a note to say that I loved him, and placed my wedding ring on the note. On the way out of Sydney we stopped off at my mother's place, where I told her and my stepfather that I was leaving Viggo. I borrowed $100 for petrol and drove off, crying bitterly, hardly able to make out the road through my tears. I grieved for the trust I thought I had found, for the security, the deep love that we had shared, and for the future that could have been. I could not understand how it had come to this. Five-year-old Joshua, who adored his father and understood the gravity of what was happening, asked lots of urgent questions from the back seat. When could he see his dad again? he asked, sobbing inconsolably, flanked by his sisters, as we all headed for an uncertain future.

CHAPTER 18

'No, no, don't come in, get out, GET OUT!!!' Viggo shouts at me as I am about to walk into his room. Shocked, I leave and walk over to the nurses' station. Fortunately, a nurse is sitting there, working at a computer.

'Excuse me, Viggo seems very upset and doesn't want to see me. Do you know what's wrong with him?'

'Oh, I see,' she says, and then explains that when people are close to dying, they often become agitated due to a decrease in blood circulation to the brain, and sometimes suffer from end-of-life delirium.

She goes to see him and comes back out again. 'Try to go in again and see how you go, he seems to have calmed down,' she advises me.

I walk over to his door. 'Can I come in now?' I ask.

He agrees, and then motions for me to come close. I lean in and he asks in a secretive whisper whether I want to know why he didn't want me to come in before. 'Of course,' I answer, expecting to hear something lucid. Wide-eyed, he whispers— although no one else is in the room—that someone was showing him how he could cure himself, and he didn't want to be disturbed during those instructions. I pretend to accept his explanation and ask a few questions about it, but it upsets him so I change the subject. Thankfully, he soon seems to be back to his normal self.

Later that day, his old PA comes to visit. He is very happy to see her; they exchange recollections from their time as colleagues. He becomes quite manic, asking me to push his bed out to the large kitchen because he wants to have a party. Once out in the common kitchen, he repeatedly pulls off his covers, revealing his emaciated scantily dressed body, faster than I can manage to cover him up again. Fortunately, his PA understands the situation and is unperturbed. Eventually she leaves, and I push Viggo back to his room. He settles and is soon asleep. The dinner cart comes by and I wave them away, having accepted that he is no longer interested in eating. I sit back in my vinyl chair and think back to that traumatic time when I and the children left him.

*

I was devastated about the end of my marriage to Viggo, and could not fathom how it had happened. How he could be so cold and uncaring about the needs of our children, about me. I could not understand what had happened to our deep commitment, and now questioned the veracity of those tender loving moments we had shared. Although it was I who had left, I felt he had given me no choice. I felt vulnerable, ashamed that I had been tricked somehow into baring my soul, deeply wounded, and abandoned.

I had no idea where this journey with the children would lead me. I just had to trust that it was the right thing to do. We were hardly out of Sydney when a large truck swung in front of my car, and that was when the magic began. Driving behind it, I noticed a large advertisement painted on the back: 'Kismet Removals'. At first it didn't register, but then I remembered the message during my meditation, 'Kismet is true.' Despite my heartbreak, I instantly felt safer. Somehow, I was being shown that I was doing the right thing and I just needed to trust the process, although I had no idea how we were going to survive.

After six weeks away with the children in Queensland, I consulted a lawyer and then sent a letter to Viggo to let him know that we were returning to the house. The tension was palpable upon our arrival and continued until I successfully found alternative accommodation a couple of weeks later. It was actually Rebecca who found it for us. She suggested that I call her grandfather, Michael's father, who lived alone in a large house in Willoughby. The house had two separate areas, making it possible to share it between two families. There I was, no longer his daughter-in-law, but asking to share his house with me and my children after spending years refusing to live in his house. I knew he had always liked me, and to my relief he agreed. So, although I could hardly believe the whole unlikely situation, we moved in. As the old man showed me to my bedroom, I noticed a pile of plastic bags lying on the double bed. I picked them up, handed them to him, and noticed the brand name of the bag on top of the pile. It was Kismet. I was shocked and spooked, but strangely reassured that although the situation seemed to be completely crazy, it was somehow meant to be.

As the weeks progressed, it became clear that the old man was very sick and in the process of dying. Shamefully, I remembered back to my earlier immature and selfish attitude. This certainly seemed like karma if there was such a phenomenon. When the children were in bed, the old man would sometimes join me in the common kitchen and confess his sins, wanting to get it all off his chest. Strangely, crazily, we somehow became a 'we', and towards the end I even washed his clothes, thankful for the chance to show my gratitude and make amends.

In the meantime, I had left no stone unturned in my attempt to get custody of the children. I wrote to Gilla, asking her the exact details of Viggo's nervous breakdown. My intention was to use the information as evidence in court so I could prove that he was unfit to have main custody of the children. I never heard back from Gilla, but Viggo did, unbeknown to me. I found a copy of his handwritten reply to her more than 30 years later:

12/3/1987
Dear Gilla, I received your letter today. I say
'I' received your letter, because you had
written both our names on the envelope. At
first I thought that something terrible had
happened, next I thought that you or one of
your friends wanted to come to Australia and
that you therefore tried to get in touch with us.
As I was in the process of opening the envelope
I thought, yeah, there is plenty of space here to
have a few people stay—I will return to this
fact later in my letter.

Then, when I started to read your letter, I
did not understand a word of it—I had to read
the letter several times—and then I discovered

that the letter was not addressed to me at all, but to Mimi.

And very slowly I began to understand that Mimi must have written to you to seek information about my nervous breakdown in 1975. My God, it is more than 10 years ago.

And why—why—yes, I will tell you how this came about. Briefly, both Mimi and I have and are deeply involved in the study of supernatural phenomena—meditation, dream analyses, personal growth and research of our entire existence—a big mouthful—we have both arrived at the view that there is a higher power—God, if you will, or the Everything, or the Light etc., call it what you choose, we both feel that we can come into contact with this 'energy', especially through meditation. Besides, Mimi believes that we are reincarnated and that we both have lived before in another situation and time. Here our beliefs part company in that I accept that reincarnation is a possibility, whereas Mimi is convinced that the phenomenon exists and that she has experienced situations where she can steer herself back to these earlier lives.

Here things start to get out of control.

Now we will go back to the time when Nicola, our now 10-month-old daughter, was born and the time just prior to her birth. It is not wrong to say that Nicola wasn't planned—and when we became aware that Mimi was pregnant we were at first both depressed. Since that time I became really happy and began to look forward to our little new one. In the meantime Mimi continued to be depressed and our relationship was affected—especially as I felt that we had been hit hard financially. We attended counselling to straighten this out. Mimi has always wished that we could live in the country and create children, and just be together all the time. I am more practical and my habit is to plan things before acting.

We agreed to work on trying to both get what we wanted, perhaps live close to a town so Mimi could live in the country and I could continue my work as architect.

In the meantime Nicola was born and I decided to look for a new and better-paid position.

Mimi was still depressed and the doctors explained it as 'post-natal depression'. We are now going forward to the time around Christmas, or at least December—Mimi wants to go on a holiday—and I say we can't afford it. This creates a whole lot of friction, and I decide to take 2 weeks off around Christmas to be with the family.

In the meantime it doesn't look like we will have a whole lot of time with one another as Cassandra, Mimi's oldest daughter, comes to stay for Christmas—she has lived at her father's in Canberra during the past year. Mimi's brother also decides to arrive for a visit and so does one of Mimi's friends, Edith, whom she hasn't seen in 7 years. Edith is divorced and lives on a farm in Queensland with her children.

It is now Christmas, and it feels as if I am at the Rådhuspladsen in peak hour. People come and go—suddenly Edith's 3 children arrive, and people sleep on the floor on the balcony. Chaos.

Our relationship is now very tense and Mimi declares that she intends to move to the country with Edith and start up a commune. At first I agree with this idea, but then realise how irrational this is. Mimi wants us to sell the house one day and then changes her mind the next, then she wants a new car.

Things are quite chaotic and we are unable to speak with one another—and at the same time I have a feeling that she just wants to get away from me.

To summarise a long story. It all ends with Mimi moving out with the children one day when I'm at work and I have no idea where in the world she is, finding out as time goes by that she has gone to Queensland and lives in an old caravan. Since then she moves to her friend's farm and calls me one day to say that she intends to come home only to gain custody over the children.

She has been here for 10 days whereupon she left the house again while I was at work. She emptied the house of furniture so that all I have is my own bed and a table and a chair.

At the time of writing I do not know where she is or where my children are.

It hurts—and I love Mimi and she loves me, we just can't live together, because I have decided not to be a door mat any longer and am actually able to stand by and say no. We cannot continue unless Mimi changes her behaviour and I think she can see this but will not admit it to me.

I don't know what Mimi has written to you and how she wants to use this information—I can only guess—and I do not like what I'm guessing.

Briefly I just want to tell you that I have at last settled here after many years and have created friends. Mimi and I have two wonderful children, Joshua 5½ and Nicola 10 months. Rebecca is 13 and Cassandra 15. I live in a house north of Sydney which I have designed myself—I can tell you it has its problems—and as I said, there is now a lot of empty space here. The house is situated on the edge of the bush, which is very beautiful. The house sits on a hill and has been built as a pole house, with the poles cemented into the bedrock.

I am working for a very large architect firm and run my own projects. It is exciting to work as architect here, but the quality is not as high with regards to the product, although that is slowly changing. We are building glass buildings nowadays and that is quite exciting.

Yes, so things are going well on the one hand and not at all on the other. It will probably be difficult to come to an understanding with Mimi following all this pain—although I will leave it to a higher power—and at the same time work on myself to try to understand what I am doing wrong since it is now my second marriage that is going into dissolution.

I believe that it is clear from my letter that I am completely 'normal'—whatever that is—and that I am neither committed nor intend to be committed to a psychiatric hospital.

With regard to Mimi, I am very concerned, but I can't help because she doesn't want any help. I can therefore just try to work myself out and change my behaviour towards Mimi and through this force her to look at herself.

In the end, we only have ourselves, regardless of loving and being loved by however many others. Without self-acknowledgement and understanding of one's own background and why we behave as we do, we remain children and play games with one another, which hurt and are destructive.

In between all my despair I understand that I must live through these things in order to become a better—and more grown-up—person. I believe we came to this earth to learn to live with one another in peace and love. When we have learnt this, our mission is over. So, if I am still alive—and I am—then it must be because I still have something to learn.

It is not an accident that these circumstances have led me to a situation where I sit and write to you at a time when my relationship to another woman is breaking up, the same woman who was the reason that our own relationship had to end.

*And now as I am writing I know, too, that this is precisely **not** the reason—but a much deeper underlying reason—which is predetermined from the beginning of existence. A road that has been determined so that we can learn to live, become cleaner, more polished, before we return to where we came from.*

I will finish here, Gilla, in the hope that your life will form itself beautifully, rich in love and understanding.

Love, Viggo.

*

It was clear from Viggo's letter that he thought I was rock solid in my belief about reincarnation. And while it was true that I did experience some events during the courses and through meditations that seemed to point that way, I was too sceptical to be gullible, and always kept an open mind. He also seemed to believe that I was depressed because I had not wanted another baby. This was entirely untrue. I had very much wanted another baby, but when I did get pregnant amid our stand-off about contraception, I felt guilt and shame at my part in letting the pregnancy happen, especially at my mature age. The depression came as a result of Nicola's feeding problems and my repeated occurrences of mastitis, which then deepened due to Viggo's emotional abandonment and disdain at my 'weakness'.

I read with interest that Viggo blamed my mental state on the breakdown of our marriage, never once mentioning his own role. Abandonment was a weapon we were both adept at using against each other. It was *the* barrier that crept back time and again, preventing us both from staying committed. I needed to feel free to leave; it was my defence against being abandoned again. And fear of abandonment was also the reason Viggo, aged 16, broke off with me and lied that he had met someone else. He could not bear to be left, like he had been left in the orphanage, and by his father's death. We both needed to be the first to leave in order to defend ourselves. As an adult I had left him in Denmark on two occasions before we both eventually committed to our relationship, and now when I was finally committed, he had made it impossible for me to stay.

I was heartbroken and felt hopeless, gutted, disillusioned. Having opened my heart, having allowed my maternal dependency on a man to surface, I had been cruelly rejected, shut out, and discarded. Yet, I somehow mustered a steely will to follow the plan of escaping with the children, and it paid off. I succeeded in gaining main custody so that the children would live with me, while Viggo had access every second weekend. Sometimes he did not turn up to collect the children, and I felt Joshua's pain and disappointment—he always waited for Viggo eagerly—remembering similar occasions in my own childhood. In between our silent wars we tried to be civil and even reached agreement about the details of our separation. I knew that the relationship, as it was, had to end, but my love never wavered and I kept hoping that Viggo would wake up. One day I missed him so much, I called him just to say that I loved him, and then quickly terminated the conversation. Sometimes he would ask to visit the children outside the times of the custody boundaries. I agreed to this, and when the children were in bed, we would give in to the desperate yearning we felt for each other. But nothing was resolved, and there were no strings attached.

The property issues settled quickly. The house was sold and I exchanged the money for gold coins and stored them in a little elongated red velvet jewellery pouch. A few months later I allowed Joshua to travel with Viggo to Denmark for a holiday, and used the time to drive out with 18-month-old Nicola in the baby seat for a reconnaissance, looking for the country property of my dreams that was to become our new home. I had the pouch with the gold coins firmly in my pocket to give me confidence while negotiating with real estate agents, who might not otherwise have taken a single mum seriously.

I had made a list of what I wanted. The property had to have green rolling hills and a creek, and a cute little white country cottage with a green roof. I marked a few places that looked promising on the map on the way to Queensland, where I was going to visit my friend Edith for Christmas. My first stop was Edith's mother's place in Armidale. As she busied herself making up a bed for me, she pulled out a blanket from its plastic case. At the front of the case was a piece of cardboard with the name of the product, and yes, the name of the blanket was Kismet!

One of Edith's brothers still lived at home and while we ate dinner, I described what I was looking for. He suggested that I drive out towards Dorrigo, a little more than an hour from Armidale. That night, snug under my Kismet blanket, I dreamt of a fertile newly ploughed field of lovely dark soil, with a halo of sprinkling watery mist above the dark rows. I took the dream as a sign, and the next morning I followed his advice and drove towards Dorrigo, instead of taking the route I had planned. The landscape along the road was typically Australian, dry country with eucalypts on either side of the road. It certainly wasn't the type of landscape I was looking for. Then the road turned, and suddenly before me was a spectacular vista of lush greenness on huge, bulging, volcanic, rolling hills as far as the eye could see. It was like entering Heaven. Although I was not religious, the thought immediately struck me that this was God's country. I patted the pouch with the coins in my pocket when I finally reached town and parked in front of the estate agent. There, displayed in the window, was the property I had yearned for, our new home situated 20 minutes outside town. It was difficult to convince the agent to show me the house. He thought a single mum should not live in such an isolated place, but he finally relented and took us out to see it.

Securing a loan without a job was the next challenge, and at one stage the property was also withdrawn from sale. But I believed that it would be mine, and five months later I was the owner of 16 acres of regrowth rainforest overlooking a misty valley. One acre was cleared with a half-finished house. It was a settler's cottage, neither cute nor white, but I was ecstatic and could not believe my luck. While my property negotiations were underway, Viggo and I had our day in court over custody, flanked by our lawyers. Viggo and his lawyer wanted to prevent me from moving to the country with the children. The judge dismissed the objections and sided with me, and in an instant the case was over. I was free to move to Dorrigo with the children. Viggo and I left the lawyers to sort out the details, stepping out of the courtroom at the same time. We stood together in silence, waiting for the lift.

In the lift he turned to me. 'Would you like a cup of coffee?'

I had so hoped that he would ask me. 'I would love that,' I said.

Once downstairs we headed for the nearest café. I loved him. He had no idea just how much!

CHAPTER 19

The doctors file into the room to give Viggo an overview. Doctor Death looks particularly determined. They cannot see any improvements, the trial medication has not made any difference to his condition, and there is no real reason to continue with the treatments. I stare stiffly at them, concentrating, afraid of missing any details. They set out various options and timelines, and Viggo asks a few questions. What if he is thirsty? They will provide a spray—it's really only the mouth that registers thirst, and the spray will relieve it. How will it all happen? They reassure him that he will be provided with ample medication, and additional doses can be administered if needed. He will slip into an induced sleep and will not suffer.

Again, things happen very quickly once the doctors leave the room. Two nurses enter with various bits of medical equipment. More lines, more bits to be attached, this time to his lower body.

Josh clearly couldn't face what is happening here and has taken his family on a brief holiday. Nicola is back at work. I FaceTime them straightaway, hoping I can contact them before the medication takes effect. Luckily, they both pick up. I explain what is happening so they can say their goodbyes. I try to swallow away a lump in my throat and wipe away the tears with one hand. Holding up the phone for Viggo with my other hand, I recall the bike shed dream he told us about, when doctors would remove all the 'metal supports'.

Then we are alone again, Viggo in the forbidding, cold, high, metal hospital bed, and I, sitting as close beside him as the rungs of the bed will allow. I look into his eyes, as I've done a thousand times before. It is impossible to imagine life without those eyes looking back into mine. I hold his hand and watch him drift off. With no future to plan for, my mind slips back to those first few months in 1988 in beautiful Dorrigo.

*

Cassandra and Rebecca had decided to stay with their father. With great trepidation and downright fear, I cashed in my life in Sydney for my dream life in the country, raising children and chickens. Country life brought many new challenges while the children and I became established on our breathtakingly beautiful small sloping property. But despite the excitement of this new life—organising an adequate water tank, finding local workers willing to line the internal walls, employing a carpenter to build a kitchen and a bathroom according to plans Viggo had generously drawn up for me, splitting wood to feed the fireplace—my heart bled for Viggo. The divorce papers arrived soon after we moved in and I could not understand when or why our relationship had broken down, how it had come to this. Viggo sometimes wrote, called, and occasionally came to stay for the weekend to see the children. There were still feelings between us but we did not explore them, as there was no point. Viggo lived in the city, I lived in the country, and we were divorced.

Friends came to visit, but mostly I was alone with the children. I often lay down and cried when Josh was at school and Nicola was having her nap, my face turned to the wall, wishing myself dead. Small children have many needs, however, so I couldn't just lie there and wish myself away. I had to make an effort so I joined the local playgroup, went shopping, and cared for the house and the children. I made friends with some local mothers and slowly, very slowly, created a new life on the misty mountains, where I hoped to keep my heart open, heal my wounded soul, and develop my femininity further. I battled the acre of grass with a lawnmower. Exhausted but exhilarated when I won that battle, I would lie spread-eagled on its crewcut and feel the heartbeat of nature under the dome of a deep blue sky. I thought back to my conversation with Viggo in Denmark about lawnmowing. How cynical to find myself doing this now on a whole acre, and loving it!

When I wasn't busy with the children or attending to the property, I wrote songs and played my guitar, meditated, and explored world religions in order to better understand life. I read a book, Sondra Ray's *Pure Joy,* and was impressed by the way she discussed the subject of immortality. She argued that this could be achieved through healing our relationship with ourselves, as well as with others. I tacked up a poster in the bathroom that urged me to 'believe in miracles, they happen every day'. In the meantime, Viggo had joined an environmental organisation in Sydney. The members wanted to establish a commune in the country.

On Viggo's next visit, he enthused over the organisation. He also told me he felt ready for a new relationship, and had started noting down a list of attributes he wanted in his next partner: 'Beautiful, intelligent, someone who loves my children ...' He said that as the list grew, he realised he knew that person and she already lived in the country. He admitted he had wanted to rid himself of me, and had attempted this at a rebirthing therapy process he had attended, where he imagined himself cutting an invisible cord between us. As he attempted to cut the cord, he saw it turn into solid gold, which could not be severed. We each talked about our recent inner journeys, and discovered that we had both been exploring the concept of immortality. He looked at me tenderly, told me he loved me, and asked me to join his environmental group and embark on the exciting shared purpose together. There was nothing I wanted more. Again, we had found each other in the same space at exactly the same time. But there was a history of hurt between us, things that had happened both before and after our separation, and a massive mountain called 'trust' that we both had to conquer.

When the children were in bed, we ran a bath in the tiny bathtub, sat in it facing each other, and took turns confessing and forgiving all the things we had said and done to each other that would otherwise stand in the way of our new commitment to be together again. When we had exhausted all our transgressions against the relationship, we got out of the bath and made tender, passionate love, floating in unison over and over, until we fell asleep in each other's arms entirely satiated, just before dawn.

*

The children and I moved back to Sydney, with Viggo, into his one-bedroom bachelor pad in Mosman. He had bought the unit with his share of the proceeds of the sale of our home. It was May 1989. Nicola had just turned three, and our long-term plan was to eventually live in a country community with his new environmentally committed friends. I loved the challenge of making it all work. Our two children were installed in bunk beds in Viggo's only bedroom, and we bought a sofa-bed for us in the lounge/dining space.

Viggo's environmental group met for regular planning evenings and took part in public clean-up events and the weeding of national parks. I enthusiastically joined their activities. Nicola was now attending preschool while I worked in two part-time jobs. After dinner, the dining table became my desk, where I wrote another book about activities for young children, typing it on the newly invented part-digital typewriter. That was how we lived for 18 months, with a shared purpose, in love with each other and our children, despite the cramped conditions.

We visited my mother and stepfather regularly and one day soon after my father died, my mother told me that she'd had a disturbing dream. She dreamt that my father had said to her 'you are next'. Then, she saw herself in a hospital bed with lines everywhere. She wondered what the dream meant, and we discussed that it was just her mind working through the fact that her first husband had died. But we were wrong. She was diagnosed with ovarian cancer soon afterwards. I could not believe that she might die, and lent her meditation tapes and talked to her about affirmations, but nothing helped. The cancer was too advanced. My mother and stepfather asked me to write their wills, as they were both dying. I objected, saying that my stepfather was still very healthy. He said that he did not want to live without my mother.

One night, I had a dream that the sky was filled with red rose petals raining down upon me, and I understood that they were from my mother and stepfather. It was their loving way of saying goodbye. They died a short time later, first my mother, then my stepfather. My brother and I cleaned out their home and I decided to keep some glass dessert dishes, but could only find three in the kitchen cupboard. Later, as I was going through the place, I found the fourth sitting on a sideboard. It was filled with dried rose petals. And I lost count of the many bunches of roses sent by friends and colleagues afterwards.

The recession of the early 1990s saw many shops in Mosman closed and empty. A few months before

Christmas, Viggo lost his job and things looked desperate. His mortgage interest rate had increased to 17 percent. Around the same time, the environmental group collapsed following irreconcilable differences between the other members. I applied for a number of full-time positions as preschool director both in Sydney and in country towns close to Dorrigo. Viggo put his unit up for sale and sold it at a loss. I accepted a position in Sydney that was to start after the New Year, and we then moved back to Dorrigo for the Christmas break to work out what to do next. A few days later, I got a call asking me to attend an interview at a preschool, one hour from Dorrigo. On the night before the interview, we again conferred in the tub, this time about our immediate future. Architects were not needed during a recession, and especially not in the country. Where could we afford to live if Viggo could not secure a job? We worked out that a job in the country for me would be more affordable than trying to survive in Sydney, and agreed that if I got the country job we would stay and I would relinquish my Sydney position. The next day, after the interview, the phone rang as I walked back through the front door. The job was mine.

*

Warm, exquisitely tender years followed. Our new life marked a change in our roles. I was now the breadwinner and Viggo was a stay-at-home dad. He had longed to spend more time with the children when we were married, and here was the perfect opportunity. With all the personal development behind us, we were committed to being our most authentic, aware, and open-hearted selves. We shared the parenting of the children. This was new for me, as I had never experienced a respectful parenting partnership before. We played with the children, had long conversations with them, travelled with them, had family meetings to help sort out their conflicts, cooked and baked with them. We explored our acres of regrowth rainforest together and fossicked for firewood. Rebecca often flew up to visit, and occasionally Cassandra also joined us from Sydney. Over time, we built up quite a social life, making friends with neighbours and others who had common interests, hosting elaborate and delicious lunches or dinners for them.

On weekends, we took long walks hand in hand on our dirt road with the children bicycling around us, rounding us up before speeding off again. We exchanged meaningful glances as they frolicked in our private paradise. The children's cats always insisted on coming along, eventually crying miserably when they got tired. We would pick them up, only to be scratched as they nervously fought to free themselves from our arms, frightened by some unexpected sound or movement in the bush. At times, Viggo and I would sneak away to make love in our rainforest while the children were watching television. There was a trickling little creek, the smell of thick leaf mulch, and the scent of wild animals. I felt feminine and desirable and increasingly, a natural part of this rich habitat.

The inner work Viggo had done made him more open and lighter. I discovered to my surprise that he was a deep thinker and had excellent general knowledge. We had long serious conversations. At other times, we took turns to spin crazy fantasies about different new and impossible ventures, and often fell into each other's arms howling with laughter at our silly ideas. I fell in love with his mind and developed a deep respect for his opinions. He increasingly participated in and became more vocal during conversations with others, sharing the wisdom he had accumulated, and he was excellent at mediation during conflicts between the children. He was a good listener, naturally calm, and could suggest rational alternatives to confronting or difficult issues, both in some volunteer work he became involved in and with friends. As the years passed, I frequently sought his counsel, as did our children and his colleagues.

We made up a language that we named 'gunk'. We would make nasal gnk-gnk sounds to each other, together with miming and pointing that could be applied to most situations requiring communication. Sometimes, neither of us understood what the other was trying to convey regardless of repeating the mime while gunking several times. This was always followed by bursts of loud merriment such that we both ended up in tears, holding our stomachs and moaning. One time, after we had watched a documentary about the South American blue-footed boobies and their hilarious mating dance, I bought blue knee socks for both of us. Long socks, shorts, and short-sleeved shirts were quite a common mode of dressing for men when Viggo first came to Australia. He was scathing of this fashion, and always dressed more formally. So I was certainly taking a chance when I asked him to wear the socks with me. He objected but was curious so eventually put them on, and I directed the blue-footed boobies' mating dance using our gunk language until we collapsed on the floor laughing. Occasionally, when we were in Sydney, Viggo would also join me in a skip down a street hand in hand, stopping only when laughter took our breaths away. Our children would roll their eyes at our antics, convinced that we had gone crazy.

While the children were at school and I was at preschool teaching, Viggo planted fruit trees and built vegetable gardens and a chook shed. The chickens had names—they were never going to be plated.

We marked dates on their eggs so we would know when to expect the little chicken hatchlings. The children loved the chickens and spent many hours observing and playing with them. A white bunny that needed to be fed with grated carrots due to its odd teeth was the last pet addition to the family. We didn't need a dog. The noise from approaching cars and the tell-tale dust cloud above the trees from our dirt road more than adequately announced any visitor.

This time, however, also marked a very black period, as all my parents died in a few short years: first my father, then my mother, my stepfather, and finally Lili. One night soon after Lili died, I had a terrible nightmare. I dreamt that Viggo would be next. In utter horror, I screamed, 'NO, NO, NO, NO, NO!' and woke myself up.

*

Against all odds, Viggo also made time between his farming activities to try and find work. He became involved with members of the community who wanted to establish a retirement village. He also became involved with proposed buildings for an Aboriginal community in Kempsey. But neither project eventuated. As the years wore on, I found myself increasingly resentful at being the only breadwinner and annoyed at always having to struggle with our finances. With the recession over, I felt it was time for Viggo to find a job, and as architect jobs were unavailable in the country, he finally accepted a position back in Sydney as architect for a local council below the Blue Mountains.

Our children were both settled in schools and I had a good job, so Viggo and I commenced a five-year-long commuter relationship. He was unhappy about having to live alone in Sydney and travel to visit us. To compensate, we both enrolled in master's degrees, and spent our lonely nights studying. He told me again and again that living apart felt meaningless and frequently asked me to remarry him. I felt safe with the status quo, and eventually confessed to him that I was scared he would become controlling again. He promised that he had changed, but I had my doubts. The children also missed him, although he visited fortnightly and called them to say goodnight every evening. They always cried when he left for Sydney after our weekends together.

In the end, the solution came with the passage of time. Josh completed high school and his needs could no longer be addressed in the country. He joined Viggo in Sydney to attend university, and Nicola found it very isolating living alone with me. She was a gifted and sensitive little soul, and was subjected to severe bullying by the other students. The school was unable to solve the issue, so I applied for a job in Sydney and in the year 2000, we joined Viggo and Josh.

CHAPTER 20

Viggo bought a house for us near Nicola's new high school where she settled in well, and Josh moved to student accommodation to be near his university. Viggo and I had both finished our master's degrees, and I had taken up studies in postgraduate psychology. I was working full time in an administrative role and was ambitious to achieve more, now that my youngest, the only child still living at home, was in high school. A year later I was offered a coveted public service position.

Despite his best efforts and promises, and although Viggo appeared to have changed, now that we were back under his roof, he became more controlling and we had occasional arguments. An example of our disagreements was the colour of the kitchen wall. He asked for my help in choosing a new colour from a large bundle of colour samples. We agreed on the shade after a lot of to-ing and fro-ing, got the paint, rolled up our sleeves, and painted the kitchen walls. I went to work the next day and when I came home and walked into the kitchen, I could tell the walls were a different shade. I soon found out that Viggo thought the colour we had chosen was not the right one after all, and without consulting me he bought what he thought was a more suitable shade and stayed home to repaint the whole kitchen.

I had kept the property in Dorrigo, just in case, and we drove up regularly to mow the acre around the house. Work, children, friends, holidays away, and occasional trips to Dorrigo made up our lives for the next three years. Our relationship took a back seat, something we now took for granted, and our disagreements mounted. One day when we had yet another heated discussion, I thought, 'This is never going to work.' I stormed off furiously and started packing. Viggo quietly called me, saying he had something to tell me. The way he said it made me stop. I walked slowly back into the lounge room where he sat down. He told me that he had asked for a blood test to check the health of his prostate, and the test had come back showing that something was very wrong.

It was one of those moments when reality assaults belief and expectations. A moment you hope will never happen. All my feistiness drained out of me and I quietly unpacked my bag. Now, all I wanted was to urgently protect him. We made an appointment to see a professor of haematology, who diagnosed myelodysplasia. There was no cure, and the prognosis was unknown, although Viggo thankfully had the least lethal type of the disease. I did some research and found that the maximum time anyone had lived with the disease was 14 years. I worked out that if he managed to stave off death for that long, he would be around 70. After expecting an immediate death sentence when he was first diagnosed, it gave us hope of a reprieve. I decided that I could live with the knowledge of that extra time with him.

His diagnosis had a profound effect on me. Now I would definitely lose him, exactly like I had dreamt. Suddenly, all the incompatibilities—the things I just could not accept, the years of clashing egos, of competing gender roles, of arguments about whose needs were more important or who had the best taste in interior decoration—lost all significance. His diagnosis marked the moment of my complete commitment. I pledged that we would 'do this together' and often repeated it to comfort Viggo. I became his fierce and alert lioness, caring for him, accompanying him to doctors, reminding him of any new symptom to report, questioning the specialists, fighting for his life. I willed my deep love, now mingled with the agony of grief, to keep him alive.

Facing the finality of his life and our time together also changed him. We became ridiculously considerate towards each other, so tender. Our love knew no bounds, became deeper than ever, immense, so precious and intense that it hurt. I was going to lose him, and grief became my everyday companion. 'You don't know how much I love you,' he would often say. 'I love you more,' I would tease.

This was the same love that had overwhelmed us when we were young; a huge and uncontrollable force that had kept us apart until we were both ready to be subsumed into it. Throughout the years its purity had dislodged in us everything that wasn't love and forced us to overcome each obstacle. Our love gave us the courage to face our shortcomings and to peel off layer after layer of past history that had barricaded our relationship; propelled us to feel every inner pain, because the pain of being apart was even more intolerable. Our love had been tempestuous and passionate, something larger than ourselves that we had gifted to each other, as inevitable as the natural merging between two halves of one soul. Our love had helped us face and rid ourselves of our demons and had healed each of us in the process. It had formed a cradle of welcoming warmth and security for our children and friends. Having come this far, it now seemed that before us was another lesson to transmute our love to something even more exquisite during our last chapter.

*

Viggo's disease was managed with medication for the first six years. During this time, Rebecca gave birth to twins. We sometimes got to walk them in their stroller and our eyes would lock, remembering all the other little ones we had looked after together. Our relationship remained as electric and exciting as ever, even more poignant, as we knew it had to end. Time and time again we relived how we had met, adding fresh thoughts and theories to our recollections, stoking our love, keeping it new. We still had time, so we drew up an action plan. Both of us wanted to travel, and the time to do it was while Viggo was well.

The first trip was to Europe, and with the issue of trust now fully resolved, I told him on a beautiful sunny day sitting in Sienna overlooking the square—an exquisitely romantic location—that I would like to marry him again. He was so happy! We were married later that year at the registry office on 14 November 2004—the 40th anniversary of our first meeting. Joshua and Nicola were our witnesses. After the ceremony, we'd invited friends and family on a dinner cruise on Sydney Harbour to celebrate the anniversary of our meeting and during the dinner, Viggo stood up to give a speech and broke the news that we had remarried earlier that day. Our friends could hardly believe it, fascinated with the romance, the tempestuousness of the relationship, and the depth of our love for each other. We feasted, laughed, and danced the night away with the people who mattered most to us. We had never before been so confident in our relationship, so solid now, so totally united.

I finished my psychology studies and enrolled in a PhD. The studies provided an 'out' for my grief and worries; it gave me a safe place, an intellectual journey away from the looming emotional threat of Viggo's illness. In the midst of my personal hopelessness, my studies gave me a curious kind of hope, that they might uncover something new. Viggo became the rational sounding board for my many ideas; a patient listener to my monologues about theories that he had heard many times before; my mentor, when it all seemed to be impossible, providing me with fresh suggestions; my editor when I wrote a section in the thesis or a journal article; my technical expert when my graphs would not behave. We would often sit up in bed and contemplate a sentence, or discuss an idea while sipping our early morning cup of tea. We would discuss a variety of options on our morning walks. At night, I would slip out of bed after lovemaking and sit at the computer until long into the small hours.

My studies became a welcome distraction for us both over the next seven years, as they were marked by some shocking health emergencies. First, Viggo's spleen swelled until it had to be removed. This was followed a few days later by blood clots in his lungs when he almost died during a three-day stay in intensive care. Joshua went to visit him and said he was not ready to lose him yet. After this, Viggo rallied miraculously and we continued our lives, our work, and travels. In between there were major family milestones: celebration of the conferment of the children's degrees; the first few birthdays of Rebecca's twins; Rebecca's wedding, and eventual separation; and Joshua's wedding. In the meantime, we regularly saw specialists who were readying Viggo for stem cell transplant, an innovation that promised to prolong his life, although he had a poor long-term prognosis.

Then Viggo had two strokes, which severely affected him. His illness took a serious turn for the worse. He became very weak, and I could hardly wait for an appointment with the specialist so that he could be booked in for the stem cell transplant. When we arrived for the appointment, the specialist was not available after all. I refused to leave and asked to see his superior, the professor. I kept insisting and eventually I was told that the professor would see us, but only for a moment. Once inside his rooms he took one look at Viggo and said he didn't think Viggo would last until Christmas. I pleaded for him to approve the transplant. As there was not much to lose, he finally agreed. So after nine years of illness, Viggo received a stem cell transplant. Another stroke and many other medical emergencies soon followed, but Viggo lived to fulfil his greatest desire—to see his own grandbabies, Joshua's two little girls. He needed to know that he, and we, would continue. He needed to experience the physical manifestation of our immortality.

CHAPTER 21

The palliative care unit has its own life. Relatives and visitors come and go; doctors and nurses periodically walk in small groups along the corridor, moving their computer trolley along; food trays pushed by friendly attendants rattle by; mornings become lunchtimes, and then it is night-time again. At times, the door to a patient's room is pulled in tightly, and a neatly folded white sheet is hung from the top of the door, like a flag, ominously remaining that way for days.

In room number 16, Viggo's condition is such that, after telling the doctors on his second day that he intended to walk out of here, he is now lying in an induced deep sleep, his mouth wide open and opening a little more with each gasping, deep breath. I watch him in a panic. His eyes are half open and rolled back, ready for the death-monster that he has feared so. Occasionally, I walk over from my seat to kiss his forehead and face and stroke his head, something he always found calming during his long illness. Sometimes I dutifully talk to him, as I am told that hearing is the last sense to go.

Our daughters have taken time off work to be with us all day. They sit and chat, eat, cry, or wait silently with us. Our son is due from interstate.

Another day goes by, and it is 11 o'clock in the morning. Nicola arrives and Rebecca is expected a little later. Each of Viggo's laboured breaths is now followed by ever longer pauses. My eyes are fixed on his frame under the blanket, watching and waiting for the next rise. I stroke his head, while Nicola holds his hand. She whispers to him reassuringly that she and I will look after each other. Then he takes his last breath, leaving an endless silence.

*

I now wake up each morning only to realise with dread that he is dead. Unable to accept it, I look for him everywhere. Having long abandoned my search for meaning during years of study, I now return to the spiritual literature to read again about life after death, trying to find some evidence to support my hope of finding him somewhere, anywhere. I cannot believe that he is NOWHERE, but I can't find him, and I am devastated that he has left me behind. I think about death. My health, which was neglected while I focused on his, is now under scrutiny by various specialists, who each find a litany of mild disorders. I am exhausted all the time, I have no energy. I wake in the middle of the night and can't go back to sleep, then sleep half the day away, hoping to meet him in my dreams, only to wake up disappointed. I can't think of a reason to go on living, despite the children reminding me that I am much needed.

I am broken.

Then Rebecca and I take a reconnaissance trip to Hawkesbury River where we have all agreed to spread Viggo's ashes, as he requested. Our plan is to wait until his birthday on the 16th of March, the day he would have turned 70. Rebecca and I identify a couple of promising spots where boulders lead further out into the water, better lending themselves to the spreading of ashes into the river.

Having achieved our grim scouting goal, we retreat to a nearby hotel for lunch to cheer ourselves up. We place our order and talk while we wait. I tell Rebecca how I am looking for signs from Viggo. I tell her about my many conflicting thoughts about death. Some days I think it is the end. Other days I believe we continue to live forever.

'But I haven't felt Viggo's presence at all since he died. Perhaps there is no life after death, after all,' I say sadly.

She looks up at me, and then suddenly looks beyond me. 'Look!' she says, her eyes brimming with tears.

I follow her gaze. She is looking at the metal stand with the table number we were given when we paid for our meal. The number is 16.

I return home and see that there is an email from one of Viggo's old Danish classmates, Hans, who usually arranges their class reunions. Viggo always joined these whenever he was in Denmark, and I had written to Hans to let him know that Viggo had died. Hans's email sets out in detail how he is organising a class reunion to celebrate Viggo on his birthday. I write back, thanking him. I tell him about the family's plans. I also tell him about the strange coincidence of our table number.

The next day, Hans emails again. There is a photo attached. I wonder as I open the email why he is writing again. He writes that shortly after reading my email, he and his wife went out for a coffee. The photo shows the table number they were given.

The number is 16.

Author's Notes

Although this is my personal memoir with a focus on the relationship I shared with Viggo, it is partly a co-authored memoir. During the last years of Viggo's life, we discussed sharing the histories that shaped us and thereby our relationship. Prior to his death, Viggo wrote about how we met. He also transcribed our long recorded discussions and analyses of our relationship; and when he was too sick to type, he dictated additional recollections and thoughts both to me and to Rebecca. In these pages I have stayed true to Viggo's writing, recollections and thoughts so that the story of our love could be told from both sides. We aimed to unearth the truth about why we had so many false starts; what caused our relationship failures; and what factors were involved in our

Author's Notes

commitment to finally own and embody our love for each other, a love that can best be described as a wild force of nature. Through exploring our own story, we hoped to happen upon and share the magic formula for all love relationships. Amongst it all has been the mystery of the initial attraction: the magnetic pull of a strange combination of our childhoods as well as yet-to-emerge future experiences that drew us together like matching pieces of a jigsaw when we first met.

One of Viggo's childhood memories that slotted into one of my jigsaw pieces was our shared emotional trauma of the Hungarian Revolution. Watching the fighting in the streets unfold on television affected Viggo greatly, creating in him a dread of death and an urge to help protect the vulnerable Hungarians he saw. I, a Hungarian refugee, was the living link to that experience and in his mind, I needed protection. There was also the Australia connection, something that revealed itself later. His family had planned to emigrate to Australia when he was four years old, but the plan was eventually aborted. A few months after I met Viggo, I left Denmark for Australia.

For me, brown eyes like Viggo's were high on my teenage wish list in potential boyfriends, most likely because my mother had brown eyes. As a 15-year-old, my assessment of a potential partner was very superficial. Besides brown eyes, Viggo dressed like

Author's Notes

The Beatles, and I was besotted with the band at the time. I used to listen to their records constantly while gazing at posters of The Beatles that adorned my bedroom walls. Paul McCartney was my favourite, and he had brown eyes. So Viggo, with his Beatles haircut and high-heeled boots, fitted in perfectly with my teenage idolisation.

Viggo's mother Viola always had her hair permed, and as far as Viggo was concerned she had curly hair. This no doubt played a role in Viggo finding my dark frizzy-curly hair attractive, although it had previously been a constant source of much teasing by my mostly blond and straight-haired Danish compatriots.

What I have learnt about love is that it begins with an irresistible pull to a partner, mysteriously propelled by pasts and futures yet to be lived; that it is impossible to resist its passionate storm; that you must have unswerving faith in its power because it will inevitably dislodge all personal barriers; that courage is needed to heal everything in its way—even if that means giving up the relationship in order to keep it; that the timing must be perfect, when both want love above all else. And that it is a spiritual journey, because, as Viggo realised, that's what it's like when you really love someone.

*

Mimi in Denmark, aged 18.

Viggo on his motorbike holiday in England, aged 19.

Mimi and Viggo on his first visit to Australia, May 1977

Mimi's and Viggo's first wedding, 1 September, 1984.

Second wedding, 14 November, 2004

www.ingramcontent.com/pod-product-compliance
Lightning Source LLC
Chambersburg PA
CBHW021140080526
44588CB00008B/147